HOLLYWOOD JESUS

MATT RAWLE

HOLLYWOOD

JESUS

A SMALL GROUP STUDY
CONNECTING CHRIST AND CULTURE

Abingdon Press / Nashville

HOLLYWOOD JESUS
A SMALL GROUP STUDY
CONNECTING CHRIST AND CULTURE

To my daughters, Isabelle, Annaleigh, and Cecilia

CONTENTS

INTRODUCTION

What comes to mind when you hear someone refer to *pop culture?*

Maybe you think about the newest playlist on Spotify or the new releases on Netflix or the top-grossing smartphone apps. Or maybe you think of something more under the radar. Sometimes pop culture begins with a small, fanatic fan base who loves a relatively unknown book, movie, band, or artist. Maybe there's the band you never hear on the radio but everyone's talking about. Or that series of novels you think looks weird but that inspires legions of people to write "fan fiction" surrounding its main characters. Sometimes, instead of becoming trendy, these artists retain a faithful, insider following. They become less "pop" and more "cult," becoming what is known as a "cult classic."

Regardless if you picture an example of "pop culture" as an innovative hit like *Breaking Bad* or something more fanatic and underground like *Firefly*, there's no denying that the popular music, books, television, movies, and media have much to say about the world in which we live. The word *culture* is used often, by many different people in many different ways, but in its simplest form, *culture* is simply an expression of how a community understands itself. God, our Creator, supplies us with the raw ingredients of humanity—talents, time, creativity, desires, ingenuity—and "culture" is whatever we cook up. Stories, songs, recipes, traditions, art, and language are all displays of how we interpret the world and our place in it.

So what role does God play in our culture—in our day-to-day lives and in the work of our hands, which produces music and art and literature and plays and movies and technology? Throughout history, people have debated this issue and adamantly drawn a dividing line between that which should be considered "sacred" (that which is explicitly religious in nature) and that which should be considered "secular" (that is, everything else). At first glance, these may be seemingly easy judgments to make, but when we stop to examine what God has to say about this division, we might be surprised at what we find.

Scripture says that *all* things were made through Christ (John 1:3), and through Christ *all* things were reconciled to God (Colossians 1:20). In other words, everything and everyone in our world contains a spark of the divine—everything is sacred, and whether or not we choose to live in that truth depends on our perspective. For example, think of sunlight as a holy (sacred) gift from God. God offers us sunlight so that we can see the world around us. We can celebrate the sacred by creating things that enhance the light in our homes, such as larger windows or skylights, or we can hang heavy drapes and close the shutters in order to diminish the sacred and shut out the light.

Our sacred work is letting in as much light as possible, things that keep the light out need to be rejected or transfo~~rmed~~.

Through Jesus, God put on flesh and walked among us, in our world, in order to re-narrate what it means to be a child of God. God assumed culture and transformed it. So now all is sacred, and in everything we are to see and proclaim his glory. I truly believe we are called not to reject the culture we live in, but to re-narrate its meaning—to tell God's story in the midst of it. Jesus didn't reject the Cross (the sin of our world); rather, Jesus accepted it and transformed it from a death instrument into a symbol of life and reconciliation.

THE POP IN CULTURE

Sometimes it's easy to see God in the midst of culture—in the stories of Scripture and in reverent hymns and worshipful icons. Other times the divine is more veiled—hidden in a novel, concealed in classic rock, obscured by an impressionist's palate.

As we walk with Christ, we discover the divine all around us, and in turn, the world invites us into a deeper picture of its Creator. Through this lens of God's redemption story, we are invited to look at culture in a new and inviting way. We are invited to dive into the realms of literature, art, and entertainment to explore and discover how God is working in and through us and in the world around us to tell his great story of redemption.

The Pop in Culture series is a collection of studies about faith and popular culture. Each study uses a work of pop culture as a way to examine questions and issues of the Christian faith. Studies consist of a book, DVD, and leader guide. Our hope and prayer is that the studies will open our eyes to the spiritual truths that exist all around us in books, movies, music, and television.

Hollywood Jesus

One of the things that lie at the heart of the Christian faith is the ability to share the gospel story and a personal understanding of what God is doing in the world. But how do you tell someone the story of Jesus' feeding of the five thousand? This miracle is recorded in all four of the Gospels—Matthew, Mark, Luke, and John—but each account is slightly different. Matthew makes a point that there were five thousand men plus women and children there. Luke remembers that when Jesus welcomed the crowd, he taught them about the kingdom of God. Mark remembers that when Jesus saw the crowd, he was filled with compassion because they looked like sheep without a shepherd. John records that Jesus specifically asked Philip to feed the hungry crowd. Each Gospel offers specific details that are only mentioned in that particular story. So which story do you tell? Do you choose one over the other? Do you combine all four stories into one? Do you skip over the details and just say that Jesus fed the hungry and so should we?

Just as when we share the stories of our faith, when a director or writer or actor puts Jesus on the silver screen, there are decisions that have to be made. Some decisions seem pretty straightforward, such as, "What should Jesus look like?" Most paintings we have of Jesus reveal a Jesus with long hair and some kind of beard and a light skin tone. But one of the earliest pictures of Jesus, housed in the British Museum, is a fourth-century Roman mosaic in which Jesus has short hair and no beard. All of these pictures, for good or ill, are simply guesses as to Jesus' appearance, because Scripture never details Jesus' features. When Scripture becomes script, decisions have to be made—from the simple, "What did Jesus look like?" to the more complex, "Which Jesus should be portrayed?"

Though the majority of us do not work in the film industry and aren't responsible for portraying Jesus to the masses, this question is for us too: what kind of Jesus are we sharing each and every day with our world? How are we portraying Jesus to those in our circles of influence? How are they seeing Jesus through us? The good news is that the story has already been told—and we aren't called to be clever or innovative. We are simply called to continue God's story, to say yes to what God is offering us every day and to be obedient to his call.

Hollywood Jesus:
THE BIG PICTURE FROM STORY TO SCREEN

We all love a good story, don't we? Sharing stories is how we make sense of the world around us. Early in human history, stories were shared through conversation around an evening fire. This form of storytelling built strong and intimate community, but it also meant that news traveled slowly and stories were easily changed and altered as they were retold. With the development of written language, which began with the Sumerians around 3,000 B.C., a story could be recorded for posterity and shared across communities. The written word changed how we shared our thoughts, feelings, and experiences. No longer did humanity have to rely on merely remembering a detailed plot or important details. In the written word, the story remained the same...well, mostly, and it depended on whether you could read.

Even though writing a story down on parchment helped preserve its consistency, producing copies of the story was difficult and tedious work that only few could do, and was fraught with inconsistencies and mistakes. Around A.D. 1440, Johannes Gutenberg revolutionized how the written word was shared when he created the first printing press. The printing press offered reliable copies of written works, which could be produced faster and with fewer errors than rewriting by hand. Over time, adult literacy began to increase with the relative ease and affordability of books, which meant for the first time that a physical storyteller was no longer needed to communicate a story. On the one hand, written works for the masses led to amazing progress in learning and sharing new ideas. On the other, without a consistent storyteller, stories were now beautifully vulnerable to different interpretations.

The invention of the motion picture camera would once again revolutionize how people shared stories. In 1878, British photographer, Eadweard Muybridge recorded the first ever motion picture, a short (very short) recording of a galloping horse. The following few decades saw the rise of many different motion picture inventions such as the "Bioscope," "Vitascope," and "Kinetoscope," before the Lumiere Cinematographe 35-mm, 16-frames-per-second became standard. The motion picture finally hit the mainstream during the Vaudeville era (roughly 1880–1930), allowing actors to record and share performances rather than take to the road to perform live across the country. In a sense, the motion picture combined the best of both worlds—the advancements of the written word and the printing press—and offered, for the first time, both consistency of story and storytelling without a live storyteller.

Movies quickly became—and remain—a major medium through which we share our most important stories, including those about Jesus and the Bible. The first film portraying Jesus was the 1897 silent film, *The Horitz Passion Play*, and since then, Jesus has been portrayed on film hundreds of times, in and through many different

THE BIG PICTURE FROM STORY TO SCREEN

stories. In some movies Jesus is the main character, offering a visual retelling of many events in the New Testament through the eyes of their directors and screenwriters. In others, the gospel story is somewhat hidden and open to the audience's interpretation. Whether obvious or hidden, all of the movies we'll explore in *Hollywood Jesus* will offer insight into the beauty, power, and importance of Jesus' story. Here's a few places we'll look:

- *Ben-Hur* (1925, 1959)
- *The Greatest Story Ever Told* (1965)
- *Cool Hand Luke* (1967)
- *Godspell* (1973)
- *Jesus Christ Superstar* (1973)
- *Tommy* (1975)
- *One Flew Over the Cuckoo's Nest* (1975)
- *Jesus of Nazareth* (1977)
- *Star Wars* (1977)
- *Monty Python's Life of Brian* (1979)
- *The Last Temptation of Christ* (1988)
- *Jesus of Montreal* (1989)
- *The Lion King* (1994)
- *The Truman Show* (1998)
- *The Matrix* (1999)
- *Monsters, Inc.* (2001)
- *Harry Potter and the Sorcerer's Stone* (2001)
- *The Lord of the Rings: The Fellowship of the Ring* (2001)
- *The Gospel of John* (2003)
- *The Passion of the Christ* (2004)
- *The Lion, the Witch, and the Wardrobe* (2005)
- *Ratatouille* (2007)
- *WALL-E* (2008)
- *Man of Steel* (2013)
- *Son of God* (2014)

Chapter One

FROM SCRIPTURE TO SCRIPT

If you'd come today
You could have reached the whole nation
Israel in 4 B.C. had no mass communication.[1]

Picture this. You're at a reception for your parents' fiftieth wedding anniversary. All the family are gathered to celebrate, and it comes time for you to share a few words about how much your parents mean to you. Would you simply grab the nearest microphone and start talking, sharing stories and fun memories? Or maybe you'd choose a poignant poem to express your love. Maybe you would put together a slideshow of pictures that speak for themselves. Or perhaps you'd play a special song because words alone couldn't capture your emotions. Or maybe you wouldn't speak publicly at all, but would

Instagram a play-by-play of the night for those who couldn't attend the party.

God created humanity in God's image, and part of that image is the ability to share stories, and in doing so, share with the world what means so much to us. Looking back through history—through ancient texts of epic adventures, battle stories, records of families, and tales about love—humans have always seemingly had a deep hunger to share what matters most to us in our day-to-day lives. Even though the medium has changed over the years, from campfire stories to the printing press, from telephone calls to texting, from actors on the stage to actors on the screen, we continue to have a deep hunger to share with each other what matters most.

Today, movies have become a huge part of our story-telling language, with movie ticket sales eclipsing the revenue of even the most popular books. Sometimes we even think a book really hasn't "made it" until it is adapted for the screen. One of my wife's pet peeves is when she hears someone walk out of a movie theater saying, "Eh. The book was better." She always wants to say, "Of course the book was better because it was your own imagination making the visuals!" So how do we react when a movie is drastically different than what our imaginations have created? It may be simple enough to say that a movie is good or bad or funny or rotten, but what if the film's subject really matters? What about when the Bible is adapted for the screen? Sometimes it feels inappropriate to say that a movie about Jesus was simply "good" or "bad" or even "mediocre." What does it mean if you thought *Son of God* was a bad movie? Does that mean you don't really believe that Jesus was God's Son? What if you thought *The Last Temptation of Christ* was a great movie? Does that mean you think Jesus was really tempted to have a family of his own? Is there a difference between the art of filmmaking and the meaning the film offers? In other words, can good art offer a bad truth, or bad art offer a good truth?

When Scripture becomes script, it can change the experience we have with God's Word, so let's explore how the medium of film affects the way we see the person of Jesus.

WHO IS OSCAR ANYWAY?

There is no doubt that movies are a tool for communicating what matters most in our world today. Beginning in 1929, the Academy of Motion Picture Arts and Sciences gathered to recognize films that were a cut above the rest. Originally having only twelve categories, nearly three thousand Oscars have been awarded to date in categories ranging from Best Picture and Best Director to Best Sound Editing and Best Makeup. Unfortunately, categories like Best Title Writing and Best Novelty Short Film were quickly discontinued.

Oscar, the official name for the *Academy Award of Merit* since 1939, is a gold-plated art deco knight standing on a five-spoke film reel, which represents the five branches of the academy: actors, writers, directors, producers, and technicians. Oscar certainly represents the glitz and glamor of the movie industry. Oscar also seems to bring controversy wherever he goes. Best Picture winners like *Ben-Hur, Gandhi, Gone With the Wind,* and *Casablanca* have stood the test of time and continue to inspire audiences today. Others, such as *The Godfather, Rocky,* and *Forrest Gump,* have become iconic and offer memorable lines—"I'll give him an offer he can't refuse," and "Life is like a box of chocolates,"—and lasting images, such as Rocky climbing the stairs at the Philadelphia courthouse with arms raised in triumph.

Movies about Jesus haven't faired well with Oscar. Some might say that there's a bias against Christian films, and that might not be far from the truth. Others might say that Christian movies don't really offer anything to the art of filmmaking, but here I've written a whole book about it, so of course I beg to differ. Jesus' story is the greatest story the world has ever known.

HOW TO TELL A GREAT STORY

*This is the disciple who is testifying to these things and has
written them, and we know that his testimony is true. But
there are also many other things that Jesus did; if every one
of them were written down, I suppose that the world itself
could not contain the books that would be written.*
— *John 21:24–25 NRSV*

What makes a great story? Should it be compelling or funny?
Suspenseful? Heart wrenching and tragic? Or perhaps being
memorable is the big secret to telling a great story. At best, a great
story is simply a story that matters—one that offers influence and
change. At worst, stories are simply subjective, based only in personal
judgment, and thus leaving each audience to their own opinion.

Great art—whether the medium is movies or music, visual or
narrative—is something that points beyond itself. Consider the
story "The Three Little Pigs." One day a mother pig sends her three
sons out into the world to find their fortunes, but the Big Bad Wolf
is wandering about. For protection, the three pigs decide to each
build a shelter. The first two pigs, filled with frivolity and little care,
quickly build their houses—one out of straw and another out of
twigs. The third brother, more careful, patient, and wise, builds his
house out of brick. The Big Bad Wolf comes along and easily blows
down the houses made of straw and of twigs, but he is unable to blow
down the house made of bricks. Determined, the wolf then tries
to enter the brick house through the chimney, where he is quickly
cooked by the fire underneath and serves as a fine meal for the wise
and patient bricklaying pig. You might question whether "The Three
Little Pigs" is a profound and great story, but the point is that there
is more to this story than the actual tale. The story isn't about organic

architecture or the biology of wolf lung capacity—ultimately, it is a story about being prepared and living wisely. In other words, the entire tale serves to point to a truth greater than the story itself.

"The Three Little Pigs" (or as I like to call it, "A Prelude to Bacon") also provides a structure for how we understand a modern story. There's a **prologue** and **introduction**—in which Mama Pig desires for her children to find fortune and safety. The **introduction** reveals that there are three pigs that will carry the story along. A brief look at **character development** shows us that only the third pig is wise. There is **conflict** with the introduction of the Big Bad Wolf. The story **resolves** with the wolf being cooked in the chimney pot, and the story **concludes** with wolf stew and a happy bricklayer. Across genres—romance, action, sci-fi, fantasy, comedy, drama—most stories follow a similar arc. The prologue offers background, the introduction sets the stage, the conflict holds the plot, the character development makes us fall in love with who the story is about, the resolution reveals that conflict is temporary, and the ending reminds us that all good stories must come to an end.

In a way, the Gospels of Matthew, Mark, Luke, and John follow this basic story structure as well. There is the prologue of Jesus' birth in the Gospel of Luke, and the profound "In the beginning" from John's Gospel. In Matthew 3, Jesus' baptism serves as an introduction of sorts, revealing Jesus' mission to announce that God's kingdom is at hand. Then we hear stories about Jesus' character—about his teachings, his miracles, his disciples, and his healings—all with specific flavors, depending on which Gospel writer is telling the story. Conflict arises between Jesus and those who have religious and political power. The crucifixion resolves the conflict, and the empty tomb offers us the conclusion that Jesus' ending on earth was just the start of a new beginning.

But even though the Gospels do have familiar elements in common with what we understand to be a complete story, the Gospels break the mold in important ways. The Gospel of John, for example, seems completely uninterested in the normal flow of a story structure. Things happen out of order, such as in chapter 11, when we hear that Jesus is heading to Mary's house to visit with his ailing friend, Lazarus. Scripture says in 11:2, "This was the Mary who anointed the Lord with fragrant oil and wiped his feet with her hair. Her brother Lazarus was ill." The only problem is that, in this story, Mary doesn't anoint Jesus' feet until the next chapter, chapter 12. Another example is Mark's Gospel, in which the author isn't at all concerned with offering a proper ending. In Mark 16, Mary Magdalene, Mary the mother of James, and Salome go to the tomb to offer spices for Jesus' body, and they find that the stone has been rolled away. An angel appears to them saying that Jesus has been raised, and the women flee from the tomb, filled with terror and amazement. And then...roll credits. The women do not experience the Risen Lord. There's no mention of what happened after Jesus was raised. The story ends without fanfare or dénouement or a final bow of the main character.

A 1965 movie depicted Jesus's life, and billed it *The Greatest Story Ever Told*. But the gospel is bigger than a story and any traditional constraints. The Gospels—Matthew, Mark, Luke, and John— are stories meant to matter because the gospel is bigger than any kind of box we might construct to contain its truth. The Bible's testimonies about Jesus of Nazareth point to a deep and profound truth beyond the words on the page. Stories of his birth, miracles, mission, suffering, and resurrection go beyond the goal of humor or suspense—they are shared so that the world, and all that is within it, might become part of God's kingdom. As the Gospel of John says at its conclusion, "This is the disciple who is testifying to these things and has written them, and we know that his testimony is true. But there are also many other things that Jesus did; if every one of them were written down, I suppose that the world itself could not contain the books that would be written" (John 21:24–25 NRSV).

If the world itself cannot contain the whole of the gospel story, this offers quite a problem when we are called to share the story. To hand someone a Bible is one thing. To share the gospel message in your own words is quite another. Sharing the story becomes even more complex when the Jesus of the Gospels becomes the Jesus of the silver screen. When the gospel is bigger than anything the world can contain, how do you portray Jesus on film and do God's story justice? Robert Powell, who starred in *Jesus of Nazareth,* offered his version—a stoic and almost otherworldly Jesus. Ted Neely's portrayal of the Messiah in *Jesus Christ Superstar* emphasizes Jesus' more socially radical moments, with a mop of hippie hair. In *Jesus of Montreal* we see a completely different picture of who Jesus is or was or was presented to be. In *The Last Temptation of Christ*... well... we'll get there.

The gospel is certainly the greatest story ever told, though it certainly can't be contained within a category on Netflix. Even though the Hollywood Jesus is seemingly as varied as the directors who yell, "Action!" the Bible's story of Jesus defies category. To say that it is simply a great story can never contain its fullness—the good news that offers grace, demands transformation, and invites us into eternity.

How do you understand the story structure of your life? Where are you right now in your current story?

What do you think has most shaped your perspective of Jesus— church, family, the Bible, visual art, media? What images have made you feel most connected to him?

How are you shaping the perception of Jesus to those in your community or household or business?

Decisions, Decisions

Look! The lamb of God! – John 1:36b

When we share the gospel story, decisions have to be made. If you had to offer an "elevator speech," a three-minute summary about who Jesus is, what stories would you include? Would you mention the Crucifixion and Resurrection? Would you start the conversation with "In the beginning…"? Or maybe you would quote Paul, who summed up what God accomplished in the person of Jesus, saying

> [Jesus], though he was in the form of God,
> > did not regard equality with God
> > as something to be exploited,
> but emptied himself,
> > taking the form of a slave,
> > being born in human likeness.
> And being found in human form,
> > he humbled himself
> > and became obedient to the point of death—
> > even death on a cross.
>
> Therefore God also highly exalted him
> > and gave him the name
> > that is above every name,
> so that at the name of Jesus
> > every knee should bend,
> > in heaven and on earth and under the earth,

and every tongue should confess
  that Jesus Christ is Lord,
  to the glory of God the Father.
  (Philippians 2:6–11 NRSV)

When we share the gospel message, decisions have to be made. When God's Word becomes our words, we have to decide how best to communicate who Jesus is. This becomes even more complex when the words of Scripture become the words of a film script. When Scripture becomes script, seemingly unimportant details of the Gospel stories are put on display and can have a dramatic effect on the way the story is told.

Portraying the gospel story on the big screen can be a powerful tool, but it also has great limitations. In his book *Culture Making*, Andy Crouch talks about how the way we tell a story often dictates what the story communicates. For example, who said that a pop song in the 1960s had to be less than three minutes long? The record itself—because it could only hold three minutes' worth of music. At that time in history, sharing music was limited to the technology available. So it's not that a good pop song is *supposed* to squeeze in a verse, chorus, verse, bridge, and chorus in three minutes. It just had to. In other words, the media dictated the message.

So how does film affect how we are able to tell the story of Jesus? When Scripture becomes script, decisions have to be made. For example, what do you suppose Jesus looked like? In *Son of God*, produced by Mark Burnett and Roma Downey, Jesus is easy to recognize. His long hair and medium beard, along with beige robes and slight British accent, offer a typical and familiar snapshot of Jesus. *Godspell*, on the other hand, presents Jesus as a clown—complete with makeup, oversized shoes, and Superman T-shirt. I would imagine if you were sharing the gospel story with someone, what Jesus looked like wouldn't necessarily be part of the conversation. But when Jesus moves from the page to the screen, Jesus' appearance is often the first thing the audience will consider.

If you do a quick Internet search for "Jesus," the first images you will see reveal a light-skinned Jesus with finely manicured hair, neatly arranged robes, and a welcoming expression. What does it mean that this is the most commonly clicked-on Jesus on the Internet, especially when we consider that Jesus' physical appearance (other than during the Transfiguration) is never detailed in the Gospels? The oldest pictures of Jesus, such as the fourth-century Roman mosaic currently housed in the British Museum, shows Jesus with short hair and no beard, but I suspect that this Jesus would go unrecognized today. The "Google Jesus" suggests that the most commonly held picture of Jesus is one in which Jesus is a warm, inviting, white pastoral figure, ready to welcome all who answer the door upon which he is knocking. But is this a full picture of the Son of God? Hardly.

Deciding what Jesus looks like is an important element in visually communicating who Jesus was, but a more complex decision is which Jesus should be portrayed. For example, how do you tell someone the story of Jesus' feeding of the five thousand? It's a miracle recorded in all four of the Gospels—Matthew, Mark, Luke, and John—but each remembers the event in a slightly different way. Matthew makes a point that there were five thousand men, plus women and children there. Luke remembers that when Jesus welcomed the crowd, he taught them about the kingdom of God. Mark remembers that when Jesus saw the crowd, he was filled with compassion because they looked like sheep without a shepherd. John records that Jesus specifically asked Philip to feed the hungry crowd. Each Gospel offers specific details that are only mentioned in that particular story. So which story do you tell? Do you choose one over the other like *Godspell,* which more or less tells Matthew's story? Do you combine all four stories into one? In the opening scene of *Son of God*, a voiceless narrator is reciting the Gospel of John's prologue while combining images of both Matthew's and Luke's stories about Jesus' birth. Do you skip over the details and just say that Jesus fed the hungry and so should we, taking a more *Jesus of Montreal* approach?

It's not just a movie director who has to make decisions about which Jesus to portray when telling his story. Every day we make decisions about which Jesus we express through our words and actions, even though we are often unaware of doing so. For example, worship space plays a leading role in which Jesus a congregation offers. I think too often our congregations outfit worship spaces and styles in order to attract who they are trying to reach rather than Who they are trying to offer. A Gothic cathedral with beautiful stained glass windows and an ornate organ reminds us of Jesus' glory. A simple worship space filled with a few candles offers an intimate picture of Jesus. A sanctuary containing guitars and video screens presents a casual and progressive feel. Form often dictates the message. Again, it was the record that confined the pop song to three minutes. What does the form, or style, of your worship setting say about the Jesus you are communicating in your faith community? Maybe a better question is, do our preferences in worship adequately convey who we understand Jesus to be?

It may go without saying that there's nothing right or wrong about creating a worship atmosphere to meet the preferences of the people in your community. The point is to be aware that when sharing the gospel story, we each share who Jesus is in different ways. When Scripture becomes script, decisions have to be made. There is a danger, though—whether we are a big-time movie director or a small church's youth director, the danger is portraying a Jesus made in our own image rather than the Jesus of the Gospels. So, if you were to make your own movie about who Jesus was, what would you emphasize? Is the Jesus you'd put on the screen the Jesus of the Gospels, or might you project an image of yourself with long hair and a beard? Are you offering a picture of who Scripture says Jesus was, or who you paint him to be?

What kind of worship setting and style does your community offer, and what do you suppose it says about Jesus?

How are other faith communities in your area sharing Jesus' story through worship? How do they differ from your familiar experience?

How does your faith community share Jesus outside of your regular worship time?

THE SPACE BETWEEN

I have spoken these things to you while I am with you. The Companion, the Holy Spirit, whom the Father will send in my name, will teach you everything and will remind you of everything I told you. – John 14:25–26

The Franco Zeffirelli miniseries *Jesus of Nazareth* is an epic storytelling masterpiece. The costuming minutiae, the detailed narrative, and the frequent use of close-up create a screen experience that makes the audience feel as if we are experiencing Jesus' story unfolding in real time. (Watching all 386 unedited minutes of film[2] detailing Jesus' life is an immersive experience.) The average adult reading speed is around 300 words per minute, and there are 68,613 words in the four Gospels combined. So the average person can read all four Gospels in under four hours, but it takes more than six hours to watch all of *Jesus of Nazareth.*

In order to create a miniseries longer than the Gospels themselves, extra material and characters were added to the story. The most notable example of extra material in *Jesus of Nazareth* deals with why Judas betrayed Jesus. The Gospel of Luke says that "Satan entered into Judas" (Luke 22:3), but doesn't explain how or why this happened. "The devil made me do it," seems at best rather frightening, and at worst an empty and lazy excuse. Either way, *Jesus of Nazareth* spends a great deal of time filling in the gaps where Scripture is silent, which can get really tricky, especially if Revelation 22:18 is read literally—"I warn everyone who hears the words of the prophecy of this book: if anyone adds to them, God will add to that person the plagues described in this book" (NRSV). Yikes!

DID YOU KNOW?

Robert Powell, who portrays Jesus in *Jesus of Nazareth*, apparently only blinks on film once during the entire miniseries, in order to set Jesus apart from all other characters.

When creating a piece of artwork, the negative space, the "blank" spaces on the canvas, are just as important as the pastels or paint used to craft the picture. When we look at "something" on the page, we tend to forget that "nothing" sometimes says just as much. For example, how do you read the phrase "Godisnowhere"? Are you reading it as "God is now here"? That is certainly what it says, but it also reads "God is nowhere," depending on where you put the spaces. Words get all of the glory, but the spaces in between the letters are completely underrated. Spaces were written into creation right from the very beginning. When God created the heavens and the earth, an evening and a morning separated each creative "day." In other words, the spaces God wrote into creation transformed the ambiguous "Godisnowhere" to forever be read as "God is now here."

Have you ever wondered what was happening during those evenings when God wasn't actively creating the sky and sea, the birds and beasts? Scripture doesn't tell us everything we want to know. The Sunday after Easter many churches read the story of "Doubting Thomas" (John 20:24–29). Scripture says that Thomas was not with the disciples when Jesus appeared to them after the Resurrection, but Scripture doesn't tell us where Thomas was or what Thomas was doing. Consider Jesus' parable about the Prodigal Son (Luke 15:11–32). The story ends with a father's grace-filled words to an older brother who is angry that his rebellious younger brother has been welcomed home with open arms, but there's nothing said about the next morning when the two brothers woke up, living again under the same roof. As a parent, I think it would have been helpful to hear what happens next. I like to think that the father, after throwing a party for his youngest son who had returned from squandering his inheritance, then handed him a new pair of work boots and a shovel. Thank God I didn't write the story.

Some may say that knowing where Thomas was or what the younger brother did the next morning doesn't ultimately matter, but this "negative space" in Scripture, the silent parts of the story, is the space in which we live every day, isn't it? Scripture doesn't tell us what Christians are supposed to do at 2:30 p.m. on a Tuesday afternoon, nor did Jesus specifically outline work-place protocol or how a parent should act in carpool. It's just not written that way.

The truth is, we spend most of our lives as Christians improvising. Christianity is easy if someone is telling us what to say and what to do—some need denominational rigidity to simplify a chaotic world—but Christ did not come to establish a new law, but a New Covenant born of the Holy Spirit (see Hebrews 8:6–8). We are not to follow a list of dos and don'ts; rather we are called to improvise with the Holy Spirit. This makes following Christ both liberating and extremely difficult. Through worship and fasting and prayer and communion, the Spirit sweeps into our lives, warms our hearts, knocks us down maybe; but how do we live out in the real world what the Spirit is doing? In the Letter to the Romans, Paul was addressing a controversy in the church—whether or not Christians should eat meat that had been sacrificed to pagan idols. Paul's answer is:

> I know and I'm convinced in the Lord Jesus that nothing is wrong to eat in itself. But if someone thinks something is wrong to eat, it becomes wrong for that person. If your brother or sister is upset by your food, you are no longer walking in love. Don't let your food destroy someone for whom Christ died. And don't let something you consider to be good be criticized as wrong. God's kingdom isn't about eating food and drinking but about righteousness, peace, and joy in the Holy Spirit. Whoever serves Christ this way pleases God and gets human approval.
>
> So let's strive for the things that bring peace and the things that build each other up. Don't destroy what God has done because of food. All food is acceptable, but it's a bad thing if it trips someone else. It's a good thing not to eat meat or drink wine or to do anything that trips your brother or sister. Keep the belief that you have to yourself—it's between you and God. People are blessed who don't convict themselves by the things they approve. But those who have doubts are convicted if they go ahead and eat, because they aren't acting on the basis of faith. Everything that isn't based on faith is sin. (Romans 14:14–23)

In short, Paul says, "You can unless you shouldn't," which is what it looks like to live in Scripture's negative space.

Think of it like this. What do you do with a milk jug after you're finished with it? The milk jug's purpose is over. You can throw it in the trash and wait for it to biodegrade over thousands of years in someone else's backyard. There's not much else to say except that this seems rather wasteful. What about if you drink the last few sips from the carton and place it on your shelf so that it can forever be a beautiful, empty, dusty milk jug? It's appropriate not to throw the jug away, but putting it on the self to collect dust seems also to miss the point. Of course a great option is recycling—taking a now useless milk jug and creating something new from it, giving it a "new life," so to speak. Scripture doesn't say anything about recycling, per se, but Scripture does talk about Christ making all things new.

One could argue that *Jesus of Nazareth* fills in too much of the negative space, but the point is that the spaces are important. The spaces are what transforms "God is nowhere" to "God is now here." Scripture doesn't tell us everything we want to know, which is why through the power of the Holy Spirit, God offers us a holy imagination to live into the negative space. Scripture doesn't tell us everything we want to know, but it does tell us everything we *need* to know—"God so loved the world that he gave his only Son, so that everyone who believes in him won't perish but will have eternal life. God didn't send his Son into the world to judge the world, but that the world might be saved through him" (John 3:16–17).

What do you consider to be the "negative space" in your life? How is God working in those places?

Scripture doesn't tell us everything we want to know. Does this give you peace or anxiety? Why?

In what other circumstances can we use Paul's ethic of "You can unless you shouldn't"?

FRAMING JESUS

In the beginning... the grace of the Lord Jesus be with all... – Genesis 1:1; Revelation 22:21 NRSV

The Passion of the Christ, the graphic 2004 Mel Gibson movie about Jesus' last days, opens with Jesus in the garden praying to God, "Remove this cup from me." Soon Judas appears with temple guards who take Jesus into custody and begin beating him, a beating that lasts for the next two hours of film. As Jesus stands before the Sanhedrin, the Jewish priestly council, three individuals bear false witness against Jesus (that is, they lie about him), hoping to frame him for insurrection against Rome.

To "frame" someone means to create a false story, or to "set up" someone to take the fall for a crime. In general, "framing" means to create a story, to provide a structure for the story to unfold. For example, the first few words of Scripture and the last few words of Scripture frame God's story in the context of a prayer—"In the beginning...the grace of the Lord Jesus be with all" (Genesis 1:1, Revelation 22:21 NRSV). So, in a way, all of Scripture is one giant prayer. If you think about it, prayer is a conversation between God and humanity, and Scripture serves as a record of that conversation so that we might understand who God is and how we might grow in love with God and with our neighbor. What frames Scripture is prayer, and the prayer is about Jesus—from the beginning to the end.

A RECORD-BREAKING FILM

At publication date, *The Passion of the Christ*, released in 2004, is the highest-grossing R-rated film in U.S. box office history, earning $370 million.

Framing a story doesn't only pertain to the written word. Disney Imagineers also know the power of framing a good story. Many of the rides in Disney parks around the world use the principle of framing in order to tell a story. In the Haunted Mansion attraction, for example, riders sit in a small vehicle called a "doom buggy," which carries them through a mysterious mansion that quickly becomes full of 999 grim, grinning ghosts who come out to socialize with guests. As the guest moves through the ride, the doom buggy swivels so that the rider is forced to focus on only one scene at a time. First the doom buggy turns to reveal a piano that's mysteriously playing by itself. Then the vehicle turns 180 degrees to show riders a candelabra floating on its own. The story of the mansion unfolds as the ride continues down the hallway, passing a ballroom of dancing ghosts and an attic full of portraits of former mansion owners. The vehicle swivels and pivots in order to show each element of the full story so that a mood is set and a particular story is told. Like a camera that pans across a scene in a movie, the doom buggy assures that you are seeing precisely what the Imagineers want you to see.

An author uses words in order to frame a story. An Imagineer manipulates a guest's surroundings in order to communicate a narrative. A movie director uses the edges of the screen to tell the story. "Framing a shot" is a phrase used to express how a director creates what happens on the screen. It may sound obvious, but what happens within the frame of the screen is the boundary of the movie's story. Much like the covers of a book contain where a novel begins and ends, the edges of the screen are the boundary of a film's narrative. And the way a director chooses to use the camera has a dramatic effect on what kind of story the director is telling.

Especially when looking at movies about Jesus, the way the director uses the camera tells the story of what kind of Jesus she or he is trying to portray. One great way to compare the difference between each "Hollywood Jesus" is to compare the different ways each movie tells the story of Jesus' crucifixion. In *The Passion of the Christ,* the camera spends a lot of time looking down on the cross in order to emphasize Jesus' humiliation. What sets the crucifixion in *Passion* apart is the lofty camera angle used just as Jesus dies, suggesting a heavenly tear is shed as Jesus breathes his last. *Son of God* uses several close-ups of Jesus' face while he is on the cross to communicate an almost intimate "Jesus died for you" feeling. In *The Gospel of John,* Jesus is perfectly framed with a still camera shot to fit with the orderly and literal reading of the Gospel. When Jesus proclaims, "Into your hands I commit my spirit," in *Jesus of Nazareth,* the camera zooms so that the cross is almost taken completely out of the frame, leaving only Jesus' mesmerizing stare, showing that Jesus is triumphant in death.

When Scripture becomes script, the camera adds an almost subliminal depth to God's story. Shooting a character from a low angle makes the person on screen appear important and of high status. Shooting characters from a high angle has the opposite effect, making them appear small and insignificant. Shooting a scene with a handheld effect, made popular in television shows like *Law and Order,* offers a casual, almost organic feel to the story. Editing together many short "cuts" from different angles adds tension and anxiety to a scene. In all these ways, the camera adds an additional layer to the story, offering a story even beyond what's happening on the screen. It's like when you read chapters 3 and 4 of the Gospel of John together as one story.

In John 3, Jesus meets a Pharisee named Nicodemus, a learn ͜d man of high status in the community. Nicodemus meets with Jesus under the cover of night, calling him "Rabbi," or "Teacher." Jesus tells Nicodemus that he must be born again, or born from above, and Nicodemus walks away unchanged. In John 4, Jesus meets an unnamed woman of low status at high noon in the center of town. He reveals to her that he is the living water, and the woman leaves the well as the first evangelist of the gospel after converting her entire town saying, "Come and see a man who has told me everything I've done! Could this man be the Christ?" (John 4:29). Each story certainly can be read on its own, but when we put our two stories together, we see a deeper meaning. Nicodemus, a man of high status, met with Jesus in secret, in the middle of the night, and he began his meeting knowing that Jesus was from God, but still he left confused and silent. The Samaritan woman, a woman of low status, met with Jesus in the center of town, in the middle of the day, and she began her meeting in confusion, but she left proclaiming to her whole town that Jesus was the Messiah. The stories are actually inverses of each other. The subtle angles make the story more powerful

Just as the camera angle itself tells a story, in a way, our hopes, our fears, our joys and losses are a camera lens through which we tell Jesus' story. How would you frame who Jesus is? Would your camera zoom in to reveal an intimate story with Jesus? Would your camera use a wide-angle lens to show the big picture of what God is doing in the world? Maybe you're still editing your story, and it feels as though all you have is a collection of raw footage with no discernable direction. Maybe your camera can shoot a blockbuster, full of a lifetime of ministry in the church. Maybe you are just learning the ins and outs of how a camera works. Maybe you're still outside of the studio wondering what happens when someone yells, "Action!" No matter what you're working with, you have a story to tell, and God desires to hear you tell it.

If you made a short film about one of Jesus' teachings, which one would you share?

Through which camera angle do you see Jesus? Does your camera look up to Jesus, showing his glory? Does your camera look down on Jesus, emphasizing his humility? Maybe your camera zooms out to suggest a great distance, or maybe a close up to show an intimate relationship?

If you were to shoot a movie about your relationship with Jesus, what would happen in the first scene? Who might be some of the key "actors" in your story (for example, a parent, a Sunday school teacher, a coach)?

A New Gaze

Love the Lord your God with all your heart, and with all your soul, and with all your mind, and with all your strength. – Mark 12:30 NRSV

"Gaze" refers to the interaction between a film and the viewing audience—the term seeks to capture the audience's emotional response to a movie. Gaze is how we talk about a movie being moving or powerful or thrilling. It's like how a piece of music can be morose or joyful. The music itself is not emotional, but music certainly elicits emotion from us. One of the long-standing rivalries I hold with one particular colleague of mine is whether The Lord of the Rings or *Star Wars* is the better theological piece of artwork. I think it's rather obvious that The Lord of the Rings does an outstanding job of explaining the power of sin and the sacrifice needed to rid the world of evil, but my friend maintains that Anakin Skywalker's redemption

40

is the more influential narrative for understanding what Christ is doing in our lives. It's rather obvious to me that my colleague is wrong, and I find his lack of faith disturbing. No doubt The Lord of the Rings is far superior in every way.

So how do we assess meaning? How can we even judge whether a film is good or terrible or worthless as a Wookie in a shaving store? Perhaps I'm biased and my love for The Lord of the Rings overinflates my opinion of the movies' purpose. But am I "right" in my devotion for Middle Earth? Am I "wrong" for not being a fan of a galaxy far, far away? Who is in charge of what a story means and whether or not the story is good or bad or powerful or benign?

Movies are more than what happens on the screen. Film has little purpose without a viewing audience, and an audience without a film is literally a big group of people just sitting in the dark. What's the relationship between the two?

As a pastor I wrestle with "meaning" every Sunday. What does it mean to love my neighbor? What does it mean that Moses' face was glowing after he saw God on the mountaintop? What does Paul mean when he says in Romans 1[3] that gossips deserve to die (and am I gossiping about my friend who loves *Star Wars* because he is not here to defend himself)? One important aspect of discovering meaning is to consider the author's intention. In large part, the author dictates what a story means. For example, Mark and Matthew both record the high priest asking Jesus if he is the Messiah. Mark records that Jesus said, "I am" (Mark 14:62), because throughout Mark's Gospel, Jesus' identity remains hidden until Jesus himself is ready to reveal it. In Matthew, Jesus answers, "You have said so. But I tell you, from now on you will see the Son of Man seated at the right hand of Power and coming on the clouds of heaven" (Matthew 26:64 NRSV). "You have said so, but I tell you," reminds us that earlier in Matthew's Gospel Jesus over and over again offers a new meaning to the Jewish Law—"You have heard that it was said . . . 'You shall not murder' . . . but I say to you that if you are angry with a brother or sister, you will be liable to judgment," and "You have heard that it was said, 'An eye for an eye and a tooth for a tooth.' But I say to you, Do not resist an evildoer," and "You have heard that it was said, 'You shall love your neighbor and hate your enemy.' But I say to you, Love your enemies, and pray for those who persecute you . . ."[4] This doesn't mean that Jesus offered different answers or that the Gospels are contradictory or confused, but it does mean that Mark and Matthew both understood who Jesus was in slightly different ways.

Another way of understanding meaning is through the eyes of the audience. The meaning of the final scene in the Oscar award-winning *Birdman* is completely left to the audience's interpretation. One of the movie's writers, Nicolas Giacobone, even said in an interview that he is still trying to figure out what the ending means.[5] Whatever the audience interprets is what the ending of the film should be. The audience's understanding gets even more complicated when we consider artwork like the *Mona Lisa* or pieces of music like Harry Potter's hauntingly melodic title song. Without words, it can be difficult to find meaning. Can the *Mona Lisa* even have a meaning? Maybe open-ended meaning is the measure of good art?

It probably doesn't matter if you prefer The Lord of the Rings to *Star Wars*, but when a film is about religious belief, meaning, preference, and interpretation can mean a great deal to the audience. These "Hollywood Jesus" films are not just pieces of art telling the story of who Jesus was; rather, for good or ill, these films become religious statements about what having faith in Jesus means.

The "Hollywood Jesus" we see in movies is almost always controversial, for good or ill. The good news is that controversy means that Jesus still matters in our culture. It means that seeing Jesus on film still offers a powerful gaze. The difficulty with Hollywood Jesus' constant controversy is that the Jesus we see on film usually doesn't precisely match the Jesus we hold in our minds. In other words, making Jesus in our own image is so prevalent that any other image we see is unfortunately often suspect or dangerous or somehow threatening.

Part of the complexity in understanding meaning is that audiences are diverse. Think of it this way. The greatest commandment is "Love the Lord your God with all your heart, and with all your soul, and with all your mind, and with all your strength." (Mark 12:30 NRSV). We all "hear" God in four particular ways. It's all the same message, but it is experienced differently in each of us. Some of us are heart people. Heart people feel like they have worshiped when they have been moved. They leave remembering the music. They don't apologize for putting their hands up when the song is stirring the spirit within them. "Yeah, the sermon was good.... Did you hear Ben on the guitar?" Mind people are a bit different. Mind people feel like they've worshiped when they've learned something. They leave remembering the message. One of the greatest compliments a mind person offers is, "I've never thought about the Prodigal Son that way." Heart people raise their hands when they are in the moment. Mind people do the "hand-on-the-chin-lean-in." Soul people, well, they really only need a water feature and a sunny day to feel that God is near. In worship, soul people seek silence and mystery. They love prayer and communion and the holiness of worship. Strength people feel like they've worshiped when they have a hammer in their hands. They are the ones at the end of the sermon who ask the "so what?" question. They want to know who to serve and when to start.

Heart, mind, soul, and strength people all receive God's Word in particular ways. A heart person is more likely to emphasize a compassionate Jesus who healed the crowds and said, "Allow the children to come to me" (Matthew 19:14), whereas a mind person might focus on Jesus' teachings and parables about God's kingdom. The soul person talks about how Jesus went away in seclusion for prayer, while the strength person would lift up Jesus' feeding the multitudes and overturning the moneychanger's tables. Though each of these perspectives is "right," these differences unfortunately give rise to great divisions in our churches, denominations, politics, and work places.

Maybe we need to rethink our gaze. Too often I fear our relationship with Jesus is actually an interaction with the Jesus we've made in our own image, assuming that because I am a heart person, Jesus is a heart person, or that Jesus would vote for my favorite candidate. This might seem insignificant until the person sitting at the other end of the pew is a mind person and voted for the other candidate.

What kind of Jesus are we sharing each and every day in our Christian walk? The good news is that the story has already been told, and we aren't called to be clever or innovative—we are simply called to continue God's story, to say yes to what God is offering us every day, and to be obedient to his call. Because it's not about how we can construct the best Hollywood Jesus—it's about how the Jesus of Scripture can shape us.

Do you consider yourself to be a heart, mind, soul, or strength person? Why?

Can you think of a time when you had a disagreement within your faith community? How did you use Jesus' teachings to help resolve the conflict?

Which films offer the most significant gaze for you? Which movies matter the most to you?

Chapter Two

THE JESUS OF NOW...
WHENEVER "NOW" IS

I am the alpha and the omega, the first and the last, the beginning and the end. – Revelation 22:13

What are you doing right now? Maybe it's a silly question because you're obviously reading this book, but when you think about it, "now" is actually a funny concept. "Now" is hard to define, and it's instantly fleeting. It feels as though you're reading these words in the present, but the moment the words make sense in your mind, the experience is in the past. You've probably heard it said that Jesus is the "alpha and omega, the first and the last, the beginning and the end" (Revelation 22:13), which means that Jesus isn't bound by time in the same way we are.[1] It can all be a bit mind numbing, but the important takeaway is that Christ is eternal though our picture of him can change when filtered through the lens of culture.

We are often unaware of the cultural bias we project onto Jesus. Take language for example. Hollywood Jesus (the character of Jesus portrayed on film) often speaks in English, and his accent sounds more British than not. It may seem to be a small detail, and one born out of practicality, but I wonder if only hearing Jesus speak in one language influences our understanding of authority, as if Jesus is more "us" than "them"? Is this because most of these movies are written for English-speaking audiences, or is there an unspoken bias that the English language holds more authority and influence than other languages today? If Hollywood Jesus had been around five hundred years ago, he probably would have spoken Latin. And who knows what language Hollywood Jesus will be speaking five hundred years into the future!

In this chapter we will continue to explore how culture has shaped our picture of Jesus over time. The Hollywood Jesus of the 1950s, for example, looks very different from the Hollywood Jesus of the twenty-first century; and by comparing films like *Ben-Hur* with *Son of God*, we may be able to understand the cultural lens through which we understand who Jesus was and what Jesus can mean to our world today.

HISTORICAL SNAPSHOTS

I've heard that those who don't study history are doomed to repeat it. It seems that when we encounter controversy in the church, we keep retelling the story of Peter and Paul. Peter was preaching a more law-based gospel, maintaining circumcision and some of the old law's dietary practices. In his Jewish community, this was an effective way to share the gospel, lifting up Jesus' words when he said, "I say to you very seriously that as long as heaven and earth exist, neither the smallest letter nor even the smallest stroke of a pen will be erased from the Law until everything there becomes a reality" (Matthew 5:18). When Paul planted churches in Gentile communities, he took a different approach. Because preaching circumcision was a huge stumbling block toward gaining converts to the faith, Paul emphasized Jesus' words, "Don't even begin to think that I have come to do away with the Law and the Prophets. I haven't come to do away with them but to fulfill them" (Matthew 5:17). Peter maintained parts of the Law, and Paul did not. They disagreed on what role the Jewish Law played within the Christian life.

With great discernment, the leaders of the church decided that they could both preach their individual understandings of the gospel (see Acts 15, Romans 14, and Galatians 2). Peter and Paul served side by side even in the midst of disagreement.

Knowing our history helps us navigate where we are as a church. If we look back to the divisions and controversies recorded in Scripture, we might find an easier path in working through disagreements. Hollywood Jesus is almost always controversial because the picture of Jesus we have in our minds rarely matches exactly with the Jesus we see on film. Looking back over how Jesus has been presented on screen helps us understand that each generation and each director offers a slightly different picture of Jesus. As long as we are aware every picture we see is projected through a cultural lens, then maybe the controversies would subside long enough to for us to at least enjoy the popcorn from the concession stand.

BEEN-HUR

"He gave me water, and the heart to live. What has he done to merit this?"[2]

Not long ago I received a social media notification that I was tagged in a photo titled, "Matt—TBT." That could mean only one thing—that my sister had posted a picture of me from many years ago for "Throwback Thursday." If you have ever been blessed with being tagged in a Throwback Thursday photo, you'll know that sometimes it's fun to look back at the former you and the good times you've had. Then you notice that you're wearing a hot-pink T-shirt sporting your favorite band from twenty years ago. What is worse are your bangs—why did you ever get bangs? Sometimes these photos are spectacularly cringe-worthy.

Pictures are time capsules, little snapshots framing our past. Not only do pictures remind us of what we used to look like and who our friends were, but they also reveal a picture of the culture and times in which we lived. It may be easy to see that in the clothes we wore or the record player in the shot or the pictures of the cars we drove. Another clue to the photo's age is to take notice of the quality of the picture itself. There's something comforting about those grainy pictures from photo albums, isn't there? Even today, with our current multi-pixeled, all-digital technology, we often use filters to make our photos look bleached and over exposed to get that aged, nostalgic look.

Movies are time capsules too. Looking back over the years at some of my favorite films, it's easy to see how a movie is a snapshot of the time in which it was made. Watching old movies takes us back to seeing someone using a pay phone on the streets of New York or an office clerk using a typewriter, or noticing or the high-waisted pants of the 40s and the shoulder pads of the 1980s. It's amusing to see how old movies set in the future lack multi-colored displays and an understanding of wireless technology. Movies not only express how technology has changed over the years but also reflect the cultural climate of the time. For example, in 1985's *Rocky IV*, Rocky Balboa fought the evil Russian Ivan Drago, and of course Rocky won. The movie debuted at the height of the Cold War. But what if Rocky was boxing in the 1930s or today? Who would the enemy be? Or if *The Wizard of Oz* were filmed today, would the wicked witch be wicked, or maybe just simply misunderstood? If there's no place like home, would "home" be a farm in Kansas or a builder house in a suburban sprawl?

Movies about Jesus not only reveal the culture in which they are made but also offer an interesting snapshot of how the culture understood the person of Jesus at that time. The epic 1959 classic *Ben-Hur* is a great example. *Ben-Hur* is the story of Judah Ben-Hur, a Jewish aristocrat who finds himself a slave and freedom fighter against the Roman authority. In general, *Ben-Hur* offers a clear picture of good guy versus bad guy. Following the Second World War, and as the Cold War was heating up, the 1959 American culture had a definitive idea of who the good guys and bad guys were. Interestingly, the audience never sees Jesus' face in the film. It's as if Judah Ben-Hur is the face of Jesus—the freedom fighter, the victor, the charioteer who rises from slavery to victory. This picture of Jesus mirrors the postwar American cultural idea of what it means to be a child of God. We left the Depression behind. We won the "chariot race" of World War II. We were the ones to offer water to the world. It's not that this picture of Christ is "good" or "bad"; rather as a piece of art, it is fruitful to recognize that this film mirrors the culture in which it was made. In fact, the story of *Ben-Hur* made it to the silver screen twice before the 1959 version (in 1907 and 1925) and once again in 2010, with a remake in the works slated for 2016. Each different version offers a slightly different picture of the culture in which it was made.

SECOND TIME'S A CHARM

Ben-Hur was the first movie remake (originally a 1925 silent film) to win an Oscar for Best Picture (1960). It was 47 years before another remake would win Best Picture (*The Departed,* 2006).

Our language changes so rapidly. It wasn't all that long ago when "just Google it" wasn't something you would ever say. Asking a friend to take a selfie with you might get you a funny look (it still might). The hashtag used to be called a "pound sign." Similarly, the language of Scripture also offers us a snapshot of the culture in which it was written. Consider some of the differences between the Gospel of Mark and the Gospel of John. Mark, the earliest recorded Gospel, is quite short and to the point. Its brevity is partly due to its early date, roughly A.D. 60. Jesus is also quite mysterious in Mark. There's no story of his birth, his teachings are often left brief and unexplained, and the encounter between the Resurrected Lord and the disciples is uncomfortably absent from the earliest manuscripts. In a way, Jesus is mysterious in the Gospel of Mark because Jesus was still a mystery to the community in which it was written. As time lengthened between when Jesus walked with the disciples and when the stories were written, so did the stories about Jesus. When we read the Gospel of John, written several generations later, a once-mysterious Jesus now openly and often says, "I am." His identity is no longer mysterious, but openly shared throughout his ministry. And the tension between Jesus and the Pharisees that we see so often in Mark changes in John to be tension between Jesus and the Jews as a whole, likely because the animosity between Christians and Jews had grown in the first and second centuries as the Christian movement sought its own identity apart from the Jewish tradition.

If you were to make a time capsule and fill it with words and pictures to describe Jesus, what would you use? What kind of pictures would you include? In my church, our eighth graders spend a year in confirmation class, a yearlong intensive time talking about who God is and who God is calling them to be so that these youth might stand before the congregation and personally profess Jesus as Lord and Savior. At the beginning of the year, we ask them to write what they think God looks like and who they think God is. Typically the words I collect are: "I think God is big," "God is powerful," and "God is in heaven." Interestingly, by the end of the year, the language usually shifts to "God is with me" and "God loves me." It's not that these youth had it wrong before, but their words show us how their relationship with God has grown over the last year. The God who was "up there and out there," is now personal and real and loving.

In the person of Jesus, the God who was "up there and out there," became human and walked among us. It's like in Exodus when Moses met God on the mountaintop. God said, "[the people] should make me a sanctuary so I can be present among them" (Exodus 25:8). God no longer wanted to be on the top of the mountain making humanity climb toward the divine; rather, God desired to come down from the heavenly heights and abide with his people. It's the same in the Gospel of John—"The Word became flesh /and made his home among us" (John 1:14). God wants to be with us, and so he sent Jesus. In the Lord's Prayer we pray, "Thy kingdom come, thy will be done on earth as it is in heaven" (see Matthew 6:10). In other words, God wants heaven and earth to be one and the same. God's home is where heaven and earth meet, where Creator and Creation are one, where God and humanity are in eternal communion with each other. In *The Wizard of Oz,* Dorothy clicked her heels and offered the timeless truth, "There's no place like home." Though the picture of home may change, though our understanding of Jesus may change, our eternal home never changes, and neither does the company. Christ is always welcoming us into the Father's house.

What was your relationship with Christ like ten years ago? What does that snapshot look like?

What are some of the ways you connect with Jesus today that weren't around ten years ago?

What are some helpful habits you can start today for the next ten years?

LITTLE CHRISTS

Therefore be imitators of God, as beloved children, and live in love, as Christ loved us and gave himself up for us, a fragrant offering and sacrifice to God.
— Ephesians 5:1–2 NRSV

One afternoon I was walking around the house and apparently singing louder than the television, because my two-and-a-half year old came up to me, stuck her hand out like a crossing guard, and said, "Daddy, stop! That's enough." *My goodness, how rude!* I thought. *Where did she learn that?* Later in the day, my daughter was crying because the red crayon fell onto the floor (obviously), and frustrated, I put my hand up like the Pillars of the Kings seen in *The Lord of the Rings: The Fellowship of the Ring* and said, "Stop it. That's enough." In a flash I realized that I was looking into a toddler-sized mirror. Of course she learned the "stop-in-the-name-of-love" Dianna Ross hand motion from me. How else would she have learned it?

In large part we learn through imitation, observing our surroundings and then playing back what we've seen. Early in the movie *Godspell,* Jesus begins to teach the disciples about the kingdom of heaven. He says that mimicking the Pharisees' empty religious practice will keep them out of the kingdom of heaven; then he starts to pick up pieces of trash in the junkyard where he is teaching and starts to play a song. The other disciples join in making their own music based on the music Jesus had begun. Though it's not explicit in the film, the song, "Learn Your Lessons Well," from the original Broadway performance, emphasizes that imitation is the best way to learn about Jesus. Culture plays an important role in how we learn about the world, who we are, and what our role in the world might be. In a way, culture is one of the ways we express what it means to be in community. Imitating what's going on in community is one of the ways we express our desire to become a part of community. Language is a great example of how we mimic our surroundings in order to "fit in," so to speak. Imagine sitting at a table in a restaurant, and your server asks you what you would like to drink. Let's say you want a soft drink. How do you order? In the South you would probably order a "Coke." The server would ask you what kind, and you might say you want a Sprite. In other parts of the United States, you might order a "pop" or a "soda" or a "cold drink." So, if I'm in the South and I order a "pop," the server is likely to pause, not understanding what I mean. Most of us typically try to avoid that kind of social awkwardness, which is why we try to fit in by picking up and using the language we hear around us.

Culture brings us together in defining who we are. Unfortunately, culture can also divide us, revealing who we are not. It's like when you look up into the night sky. Stars clump together to form galaxies because of gravity, but the universe is expanding in all directions, meaning that the galaxies are moving away from each other. Culture brings us together, but also moves communities away from each other. Think of your faith community. I would imagine that your community, even if on a small scale, has a language unique to your community. A great way to recognize this is to read another church's newsletter. Are there terms you don't understand? Are there acronyms that don't make sense? I would bet that your community has the same. It's not that insider language is good or bad, but problems arise when I assume that my insider language is more "right" than your insider language, or the way I express myself is more valid than your way. This is part of the difficulty in diving into the intersection between culture and the church. It may be a small thing whether you should order a "Coke" or a "pop" while sitting at the lunch table, but when we gather around the Lord's Table of Holy Communion, the language we use becomes important.

Sometimes we confuse Jesus' culture with Jesus himself. Paul's letter to the Ephesians says, "Therefore be imitators of God, as beloved children, and live in love, as Christ loved us and gave himself up for us, a fragrant offering and sacrifice to God" (Ephesians 5:1–2 NRSV). We are called to imitate Christ, not imitate the first century in which Jesus lived. Admittedly this gets complex. In 1 Corinthians 11:1 NRSV, Paul says, "Be imitators of me, as I am of Christ," and then he goes on to discuss how men should never pray while wearing a hat, but that women should always wear a head covering when praying. I don't doubt that this was an important cultural distinction during the first century, but is it now? Are head coverings essential to our understanding of who Christ is? I would argue that the point is to pray and to always be in a posture of prayer (1 Thessalonians 5:16–18), regardless of whether or not you are wearing a fedora.

This is why culture is a gift, and why considering Hollywood Jesus is so important! Seeing these different films helps us understand what is essential to our faith and what can be understood simply as a cultural expression. It allows us to tell an old story in a new way for a new generation. It also reminds us that the gospel story is not about sandals and oil lamps and using a beast of burden to get around. We are to be imitators of Christ (see Ephesians 5), not imitators of the first century. The gospel is a timeless story. As the Gospel of John reminds us—

> In the beginning was the Word
> and the Word was with God
> and the Word was God." (John 1:1)

Christ is the beginning and the end even though Jesus lived in a particular place with a particular language and agriculture and traditions. *Jesus Christ Superstar* plays with this idea. In the beginning of the movie, the actors drive into the desert and reveal that they are putting on a show. The setting is Judea, yet they sing from modern-day scaffolding, and they dance among ruins and the Romans carry machine guns. It's hard to tell exactly when the story is taking place, and maybe that's the point.

Being a Christian means that we are to be little Christs. We should mimic Christ's love, compassion, challenge, and sacrifice, not necessarily his sandals, love for pita bread, or Aramaic accent. It's like the disciples in Mark 9. A man brings his spirit-possessed son to the disciples, but they are unable to exorcise the spirit who was killing the man's son. The man then brings the boy to Jesus, and Jesus says, "All things can be done for the one who believes." The man said, "I believe, help my unbelief." Jesus then casts out the demon, leaving the disciples confused. They asked why they could not cast out the demon. They were doing just what Jesus was doing. What went wrong? Jesus replied, "This kind can come out only through prayer" (Mark 9:23, 24, 29 NRSV). It was the man's faith in Christ that activated the life-saving Spirit of God. The disciples were mimicking what Jesus was doing without regard to why Jesus did what he did.

It's as if they were Southerners in an Ohio restaurant ordering a Coke, and then being surprised that they didn't get a Sprite. It is why Peter sank when he got out of the boat. He saw Jesus walking on the water, and he also wanted to walk on the water. Peter got out of the boat and sank beneath the waves. Jesus said, "You man of weak faith. Why did you begin to have doubts?" (Matthew 14:22–33). In other words, it's not about becoming more buoyant than water, but about trusting that Jesus saves.

Movies about Jesus show us that it's not about wearing a tunic like the characters in *Jesus of Nazareth*, nor is it about speaking Aramaic as the Jesus in *The Passion of the Christ*. It's not about imitating the first-century customs. It's about mimicking the love, grace, and mercy Christ offers in whichever culture we find ourselves. It's about learning the language of social media to connect with those who are connected to a computer. It's about learning the stories of the past so that those in elderly care facilities know that they haven't been forgotten. It's about sharing a soft drink with the least and the lost, regardless of what you call the drink.

What are some unique practices in your community of faith? What sets you apart from other congregations?

What are some of the ways the youth in your faith community talk about Jesus? How do they practice their faith?

Which of Jesus' teachings do you find easy to mimic? Which do you find difficult? Are there any that seem impossible?

Hero, Hippie, Clown, and Canadian

"What's the buzz? Tell me what's a happenin'."[3]

Several years ago I had the blessing of directing our church production of *Godspell*. Near the end of the production, I was very stressed. There just weren't enough hours in the day to accomplish all of the self-imposed responsibilities I was juggling. I felt that the whole production was on my shoulders and was angry that others weren't pulling their weight. I complained to one of our associate pastors about how I was feeling—that everything was up to me and no one else was doing enough. He looked me in the eyes and said, "Mr. Rawle,...you aren't Jesus Christ."

I wanted to punch him dead in the nose. I was hoping that he would give me a hug or tell me it was okay or affirm my anger by throwing everyone else under the bus. (That's why we seek out a pastor, isn't it?) Even though I wanted to throw him out the window, it is still the best advice I think I've ever received. He was right. I'm not Jesus, and neither are you. Working day by day with the cast of *Godspell*, my go-to picture of Jesus had become the joyful clown wearing a Superman T-shirt and oversized shoes, so it was a jolt to my system when I received a prophetic message that was difficult to swallow.

In Scripture we see Jesus share the gospel in many different ways. In the church we talk about understanding Christ in all of his "offices," meaning that Jesus is a king, prophet, priest, and servant. Jesus as priest is the one who said, "This is my body given for you," "Your faith has made you well," and "Lazarus, come out!"[4] Jesus as prophet overturned the money changing tables, healed on the Sabbath, and said, "Woe to you, scribes and Pharisees, hypocrites! For you are like whitewashed tombs, which on the outside look beautiful, but inside they are full of the bones of the dead and of all kinds of filth."[5] Jesus as king is the one who took the cup at the last supper and said, "This cup that is poured out for you is the new covenant in my blood," and "my kingdom is not of this world." Jesus as king selected twelve disciples and commanded them to baptize the world in the name of the Father and of the Son and of the Holy Spirit.[6] Jesus is revealed as a servant when he took off his outer robe, knelt down before a basin of water, and washed the disciples' feet. Jesus as servant took fish and loaves and fed the multitudes. Our servant Lord is the one who said, "The Son of Man came not to be served, but to serve."[7]

Jesus was comforting, challenging, full of humility and power. Jesus had many "faces," so to speak, which may be why when we see Jesus on film the interpretations of who Christ is widely vary. *Godspell* (1973) emphasizes a priestly Jesus, a clowning and comforting friend who uses stories to enlighten and challenge. He is a fun-loving and energetic teacher who you might expect to see volunteering to offer the children's message on a Sunday morning, and the disciples are almost childlike in the way they understand the world. The movie musical emphasizes Jesus' parables in an almost schoolyard-playground, vacation Bible–school kind of way. Overall, the music adds an element of frivolity and friendship.

Conversely, *Jesus Christ Superstar* (1973), also a movie musical, presents Jesus in quite a different light. This hippie Jesus is more of a prophet than a priestly and comforting friend. The music is edgy. Jesus screams at the top of his lungs, "My temple should be a house of prayer / But you have made it a den of thieves"[8] (which is just one of the coolest lines from any Broadway musical ever!). The back and forth between Jesus and Judas offers a theological depth beyond the parables of Jesus in *Godspell*—for example, regarding the character of Mary Magdalene, Jesus asks a judging Judas who he is to criticize her, "If your slate is clean, then you can throw stones. / If your slate is not, then leave her alone!"[9] During Jesus' grand soliloquy, "Gethsemane,"

Jesus asks pointed and challenging questions about what will happen after his death and whether or not his death is worth it: "Why should I die? / Can you show me now that I would not be killed in vain?"[10]

Jesus of Montreal, a 1989 Canadian film, also presents Jesus with great prophetic fervor, but in the end of the film, we see Jesus as a suffering servant. The movie opens with an actor, Daniel, receiving a meal from a soup kitchen because he is out of work. He and a handful of others are invited to offer a play detailing Jesus' life in order to raise money for a local Catholic church. When the play becomes controversial, the church seeks to shut down the performance. In the ensuing skirmish, Daniel is accidentally killed, and his harvested organs offer life to others, offering an interesting interpretation of Christ's resurrection. Finally, *Ben-Hur* (1959) presents Jesus as a king with power and authority. Early in the film Jesus offers water to a thirsty and enslaved Judah Ben-Hur. When the Roman guard comes to reprimand Jesus, he stops in his tracks. Jesus' innate authority leaves the Roman guard bewildered without a word spoken.

We must see Jesus in all of his offices: king, prophet, priest, and servant, or in this case, hero, hippie, clown, and Canadian. Understanding the diversity in the person of Jesus himself helps us understand the diversity of God's people, and the beautiful diversity found within our congregations.

Have you ever received difficult, but important advice? How did you receive this difficult word?

Have you ever had the courage to speak the truth in love? How was it received?

Which of Jesus' offices (priest, prophet, king, or servant) most resonate with you?

AN ABSURD TRUTH

"Blessed are the Cheese Makers."[11]

Mercy, grace, love, and forgiveness are central to the Christian narrative. When we receive these gifts from God, we hit our knees, our arms fly into the air, our eyes begin to tear, and we give thanks as if our life depended on it. From this perspective, a life in Christ is somewhat easy and joyful. Only a fool would reject a faith full of acceptance and love, right? Christianity becomes a bit more difficult when we are called not to receive but to provide forgiveness and graciousness and mercy and love, especially when we are called to love our enemies. It's almost an absurd thing that Jesus commands us to perform.

Monty Python's *Life of Brian*, is an absurd story about Brian, who is mistaken to be the Messiah. *Life of Brian* satirizes religious teachings, which many might find offensive, but the absurdity of the story points to important truths. For example, a crowd is listening to Jesus offer the Sermon on the Mount from the Gospel of Matthew. The crowd mistakes, "Blessed are the peacemakers," for "Blessed are the *cheese makers*." A woman asks, "What's so special about the cheese makers?" to which a man replies, "Obviously it's not meant to be taken literally. It refers to any manufacturers of dairy products."[12] It's a funny line in its own right, but it points to the seemingly endless debate of which verses in Scripture should be read literally and which are best understood as metaphor. When Jesus says, "If your right hand causes you to fall into sin, chop it off and throw it away" (Matthew 5:30), I hope you understand that Jesus is using metaphor to talk about seeking holiness in all that we do. Conversely, when Jesus says, "If you want to be complete, go, sell what you own, and give the money to the poor. Then you will have treasure in heaven. And come follow me" (Matthew 19:21), we miss the point if we don't read Jesus literally.

Admittedly, it takes a great deal of prayer and study and reading Scripture in community to wrestle with meaning, but the absurdity of Monty Python highlights a challenging truth about the arguments we sometimes get into when trying to understand God's Word.

God is clever enough to use absurdity to point to profound truth. Ever heard the story of Jonah? This familiar Bible story is about much more than a guy being swallowed by a whale. In a way, the book of Jonah is a three-act satire. Now, before you close this book, thinking this blasphemous, hear me out. The book begins with God asking the prophet Jonah to go to Nineveh and cry out against the people's sin. The Ninevites are kind of a rough bunch, so instead, Jonah flees God by jumping into a boat headed for Tarshish—that is, the opposite direction from Ninevah. While on the boat, a wild storm pops up and worries all of the passengers...except for Jonah. Jonah is down in the bowels of the ship, taking a nap. The other passengers wake Jonah, amazed that he doesn't seem worried at all. Deciding that Jonah is the reason for the storm, they decide to throw him overboard. In fact, the other passengers say, "Please, O Lord, we pray, do not let us perish on account of this man's life. Do not make us guilty of innocent blood; for you, O Lord, have done as it pleased you" (Jonah 1:14 NRSV). Jonah is supposed to be the Lord's great prophet, and it's actually everyone else who is praying to God. Jonah offers himself to be thrown overboard, which seems like an act of pious sacrifice, except it really means that Jonah would rather die than do what God is asking him to do. They pick Jonah up and throw him into the depths of the sea, but God calls a large fish to swallow him up so that his life may be spared. Now keep in mind that Jonah is trying to run from God, yet when Jonah needed him the most, God was there with him in the most unimaginable of places.

NOT WITHOUT CONTROVERSY

Because Monty Python's *Life of Brian* was protested by so many different Christian denominations, John Cleese reportedly said: "We've brought them all together for the first time in 2,000 years!"

While in the belly of the fish, Jonah praises God, saying, "I called out to the LORD in my distress, and he answered me...Deliverance belongs to the LORD" (Jonah 2:2, 9). After three days' time, the large fish spews him onto shore. The word of God comes to him a second time—God gives Jonah a second chance, asking him to go to Nineveh. With sober judgment, Jonah agrees and sets out for Nineveh. He walks into the city and delivers what must be the shortest prophetic oracle in the Bible: "Just forty days more, and Nineveh will be overthrown" (Jonah 3:4). He doesn't mention who he is, or what Nineveh is doing wrong. He doesn't even mention that it is God who is sending him. Jonah gives them the bare minimum of what they need to hear, and then he goes out of the city and sits and waits for the fireworks. Much to Jonah's surprise, the King of Nineveh orders everyone to repent and ask for forgiveness. Every resident of Ninevah is told to fast and to sit in ashes, and even the animals are included—they round up all the chickens and goats and salamanders and pour ashes over their heads. Doesn't that sound absurd?

And just like that, because they repented, God changed his mind. God decided not to destroy the city. This made Jonah quite angry, and it's quite funny what Jonah said to God—"Come on, LORD! Wasn't this precisely my point when I was back in my own land? This is why I fled to Tarshish earlier! I know that you are a merciful and compassionate God, very patient, full of faithful love, and willing not to destroy" (Jonah 4:2). Notice that Jonah is describing all attributes he apparently has trouble mastering. Remember, he praising God for his grace while in the belly of the fish, but now that God's grace is extended to the Ninevites, it makes Jonah angry.

The absurd tale of Jonah points to an absurd truth: it is absurd for us to be angry with God's grace. Grace is the greatest gift when it is offered to you, but it's the toughest pill in all the world to swallow when it's offered to someone you don't think deserves it. Christianity is easy when we are the prodigal, forgiven of our sin, greeted with open arms of mercy and love, but we can unfortunately become like Jonah, angered by what we feel to be undeserved forgiveness and radical hospitality. Jonah isn't angry at Nineveh. He is angry with God. Jonah did his job. The Ninevites did their job. God did his job. Everyone did their jobs, yet Jonah burns within himself.

We may be more like Jonah than we want to admit. We accept God's forgiveness with open arms when God pours out his mercy upon us, but when God has forgiven someone who has wronged us, we can be stricken with spiritual amnesia, completely forgetting what God has done for us. We can be like Jonah, burning within ourselves, waiting for God to smite those whom we think deserve it. That's the beauty of this story. Jonah is a satire. It is ridiculous and over the top, making fun of the role of a prophet in order to teach us a valuable lesson: we, the faithful, sometimes have a very difficult time forgiving those whom God has forgiven, fully incorporating them back into the life of the Church.

Some may find my interpretation of the book of Jonah a little offensive. Many find *Life of Brian* offensive. But, in my opinion, the real offense is the absurdity of being angry with God's grace. We are called to be a place of radical hospitality, a place where all of God's children have a place to know the love and mercy and forgiveness of God. Jesus was preaching to the crowds saying, "For as Jonah became a sign to the people of Nineveh, so will the Son of Man be to this generation" (Luke 11:30 ESV). To his generation, and to the countless ones that have followed, Jesus Christ, the Son of Man, lives for you and for me, for our friends and for our enemies. He died and three days later rose again so that we all might celebrate the grace and abundant life we have received. Sometimes the celebration is a bitter pill when we think that God is being too gracious. It's like the older brother in Jesus' parable of the Prodigal Son in Luke 15. The younger brother who spent his inheritance on some wild nights outside of town is welcomed home with grace. The older brother who was working in the field and has done everything his father asked of him is filled with rage. The older brother says, "Look, I've served you all these years, and I never disobeyed your instruction . . . but when this son of yours returned . . . you slaughtered the fattened calf for him." The father replies, "Son, you are always with me."

The older brother's anger made him blind to the blessings he had been receiving all along. He even refers to his brother as "this son of *yours*," rather than seeing him as his own brother. The scene ends with the father saying, "But we had to celebrate and be glad because this *brother of yours* was dead and is alive. He was lost and is found" (Luke 15:29–32, emphasis mine). When we harbor the idea that God's radically redeeming grace is only for some and not for all, then we become blind to the truth indeed.

Can you think of a time when someone forgave you, and you didn't quite deserve his or her grace?

Can you think of an example when something that seemed absurd actually proclaimed a profound truth in your life?

THE LAST TEMPTATION
OF HOLLYWOOD JESUS

*Since you are God's Son, throw yourself down; for it is
written,* I will command my angels concerning you, and
they will take you up in their hands so that you won't
hit your foot on a stone. – *Matthew 4:6*

Movies offer us a snapshot of how Jesus was understood in a
particular time and place. In other words, films offer us the Jesus
of "now"—whenever "now" might be. *Ben-Hur* offers a picture of
the 1950s, *Jesus Christ Superstar* is a slice of the 70s, and *Son of God*
presents a 2010 view of the Messiah. *The Last Temptation of Christ*,
the highly controversial 1988 Martin Scorsese film, doesn't so much
show us a picture of the late 80s as it offers a curious question—
"What if?" In the film, Jesus struggles with his calling as God's Son,
wandering between an ethic of love and an ethic of power. Growing
in confidence that he is God's Son, he brings his ministry to Jerusalem
and is crucified. While on the cross, he meets his final temptation—
having a family. He is tempted with coming down off the cross in
order to live a happy and fulfilled family life.

Christian doctrine proclaims that Jesus was fully human and fully
divine. Sometimes I think it's easier to consider Jesus as the fully
divine Son of God, rather than the fully human son of Mary. The
fully divine Christ couldn't have been tempted, right? Of course,
Jesus was fully human and fully divine, "acknowledged in Two
Natures unconfusedly, unchangeably, indivisibly, inseparably,"[13] as
the Chalcedonian Creed adopted in A.D. 451 proclaims. It can be
confusing, but think about it like this. When God created humanity,
God said,

"Let us make humankind in our image, according to our
likeness…"

So God created humankind in his image,
   in the image of God he created them,
   male and female he created them."
              (Genesis 1:26–27 NRSV)

What's missing? God set out to create humanity in God's image and likeness, but interestingly, God only creates humanity in God's image. Christ, being fully human and fully divine, is who offers us God's likeness. In other words, all people are made in God's image, and through Christ we gain the saving grace of God's likeness.

But *The Last Temptation of Christ* offers an intriguing question: what if? What if Jesus had said yes in the desert when the devil tempted him? In a way, he did. In Matthew 4, Jesus meets the devil in the wilderness after fasting for forty days. Three times over the devil tries to get Jesus to assume the role of God himself rather than be God's Son, the Messiah. The devil says, "Since you are God's Son, command these stones to become bread" (v. 3). Can you imagine the good we could do if we could transform rocks into loafs of bread? But Jesus replies, *"People won't live only by bread, but by every word spoken by God"* (v. 4). In others words, we need bread, and God provides bread, but even the best bread in the world isn't worth it if it is separated from God. Jesus says no to the devil's request, but later, in Matthew 14, Jesus looks upon the multitudes and takes a few loaves of bread and multiplies them in order to feed thousands. At the Last Supper with his disciples, Jesus takes common bread, blesses it, and says, "Take and eat. This is my body" (Matthew 26:26). The Bread of Life is not made from stones—it is the body of Christ given to us so that we might receive the grace of God.

Then the devil took Jesus to Jerusalem and set him on the pinnacle of the Temple, saying, "Since you are God's Son, throw yourself down; for it is written, *I will command my angels concerning you, and they will take you up in their hands so that you won't hit your foot on a stone*" (Matthew 4:6). The devil is so very crafty, using Scripture to tempt Jesus, showing us the danger of using Scripture to support our convictions rather than allowing Scripture to give birth to our convictions. Jesus rejects the devil's suggestion: "Again it's written, *Don't test the Lord your God*" (v. 7). Jesus says no to leaping from the pinnacle of the Temple, the place where God resided. But Jesus walked the earth to show us that he is the place where God lives in the world. Jesus couldn't leap from the Temple because Jesus *is* the Temple. In the Gospel of John, Jesus says, "Destroy this temple and in three days I'll raise it up" (John 2:19). The brick and mortar of his own body was beaten and crucified and was risen on the third day so that we too might reside with God for eternity. The devil, running out of options, then takes Jesus to a high mountain and promises to give him the kingdoms of the world. Jesus rejects the devil saying, "Go away, Satan, because it's written, *You will worship the Lord your God and serve only him*" (Matthew 4:10). Jesus wasn't interested in kingdoms, but in God's kingdom, a kingdom that burst from the tomb and offered life to all.

Sin can be understood as a perversion of God's first commandment—"Be fruitful and multiply" (Genesis 1:28 NRSV)—and the problem with sin is that it is half right! Sin is great at multiplying, but it is never fruitful. Making bread out of stones is half right—it ends hunger, but there's more to life than a full stomach. We may not dash our foot against a stone when we leap from the Temple; but when we hurl ourselves away from the Temple, the place where God rests, we leap away from the source of life itself. Having influence and power in the world can bring about remarkable things; but when we strive after power for our own benefit, we tell God that we no longer need his forgiveness, redemption, or grace.

There is yet one great temptation of our Hollywood Jesus—you could say that is the "Last Temptation of Hollywood Jesus." When the devil tempted Jesus in the wilderness, he encouraged Jesus to assume the role of God rather than God's Son. In other words, the devil wanted Jesus to make God in his own image. It is so very tempting to create Jesus in our own image and likeness. It's a subtle and deadly temptation. It begins when we assume that Jesus would be a member of our political party and not someone else's. It creeps in when we assume that Jesus would be American rather than Mexican or Ethiopian. We are tempted to assume that Jesus is like me, only better. Thankfully, Jesus rejected this last temptation, and we should too. Instead Jesus offered us an example of what it means to serve God rather than create a god to serve us.

Jesus suffered, died, and rose again so that we might have abundant and everlasting life with God. Through Christ, God offers humanity, made in God's image, the everlasting likeness of eternal life.

How would you summarize Jesus' temptations in your own words?

Sometimes sin sounds like a good idea. Do you have an experience of making a decision that sounded great but ended poorly? What was God's role in the decision?

In what ways do you tend to make Jesus in your own image?

Chapter Three

THE GOSPEL ACCORDING TO...

You take the blue pill, the story ends. You wake up in your bed and believe whatever you want to believe. You take the red pill, you stay in wonderland, and I show you how deep the rabbit hole goes.[1]

Now we get to have a bit of fun and ask, how far can Hollywood Jesus stretch and still be considered Hollywood Jesus? Does Hollywood Jesus have to have long hair and sandals, teaching in parables and walking around with his disciples? Where do we draw the line between portraying Jesus on film and offering someone *like* Jesus on film? There is a difference between Jesus of Nazareth and

Christ, the second person of the Trinity (Father, Son, and Spirit). The Gospel of John says,

> In the beginning was the Word
> and the Word was with God
> and the Word was God.
> The Word was with God in the beginning…
> The Word became flesh
> and made his home among us. (John 1:1–2, 14a)

Christ, the Word of God, was with God and was God from the very beginning. Jesus is the fully human and fully divine Son of God, who was born in Bethlehem, grew up in Nazareth, lived in Capernaum, died and rose again in Jerusalem, and then ascended into the heavens to sit at God's right hand. Jesus is the Christ, though he only lived among us in the flesh for thirty-three years or so.

When talking about our Hollywood Jesus (the Jesus we see portrayed on film), there is a difference between Jesus figures and Christ figures. So far we've only discussed Jesus figures—actors portraying the character of Jesus. Some movies, like *Jesus of Nazareth, The Greatest Story Ever Told,* and *The Passion of the Christ,* are retellings of the Gospel accounts. Others like *Jesus Christ Superstar, Godspell,* and *Jesus of Montreal* still have Jesus as the main character though these films aren't necessarily retelling the biblical account. All of these films offer Jesus figures, portrayals of Jesus himself. But in this chapter we will discuss Christ figures—characters who represent the teachings of Jesus though they aren't intended to be a representation of Jesus. For example, consider Superman from *Man of Steel.* He's not from earth, he has super-human abilities, he always fights for justice, and he uses his powers to save people from harm. *Man of Steel* isn't retelling the biblical account of Jesus, but Superman is a Christ figure in that he saves humanity from evil. The same could be said about Neo in *The Matrix*. Neo, the "chosen one" with super-human strength and speed, frees humanity (and the machines) from the evil computer virus, Agent Smith. Even though *The Matrix* franchise uses lots of religious language to tell a salvation story, it isn't retelling the biblical account of Jesus. So let's spend some time stretching our Hollywood Jesus definition to explore how we might understand the gospel message, even when Jesus' name doesn't appear in the end credits.

THE GREAT LION

Jesus was fully divine and fully human, but C. S. Lewis saw Jesus as being fully divine and fully...lion. Aslan, the Great Lion in The Chronicles of Narnia is a great example of how we can share the Gospel story without relying on retelling the stories in Matthew, Mark, Luke, and John. *The Lion, The Witch, and the Wardrobe,* the first book and movie in The Chronicles of Narnia series, tells the story of four young children—Peter, Susan, Edmund, and Lucy—who discover a mysterious world called Narnia hidden within professor Digory Kirke's wardrobe. Narnia is in the midst of a seemingly endless winter caused by the evil White Witch, who deceives Edmund into betraying his siblings for little more than candy. Because of Edmund's betrayal, the White Witch has grounds to execute the unsuspecting child, but Aslan offers himself as a sacrifice in his stead. The White Witch assumes that with Aslan gone she will forever rule Narnia, but after his execution, to the witch's dismay, Aslan returns. Aslan reveals that there is a "deeper magic" at work in the world when the innocent offers his life in the place of the guilty. Aslan frees Narnia from her oppression and devastating winter, and crowns the children kings and queens of Narnia.

The Lion, the Witch, and the Wardrobe is a great example of the difference between a Jesus figure and a Christ figure. Aslan is not a portrayal of Jesus, but Aslan does represent the work Jesus accomplished as the Christ, God's anointed Son. Through Aslan's death and resurrection, the oppressed go free, Edmund is forgiven, evil is defeated, and the children find their true worth. This popular movie is not a retelling of the biblical accounts of Jesus, but it is the gospel story—a story about betrayal, sacrifice, redemption, resurrection, and hope.

From Jesus to Christ

*Have you believed because you have seen me? Blessed are
those who have not seen and yet have come to believe.*
— John 20:29 NRSV

This is where our Hollywood Jesus becomes great fun. So far
we've discussed movies about Jesus, and on the whole these movies
are meant to portray the Gospels on film. Films like *Jesus of Nazareth,
The Greatest Story Ever Told,* and *Son of God* stray little from Scripture
in order to evangelistically share who Jesus was. Other movies like
Godspell, Jesus Christ Superstar, and *Jesus of Montreal* stray from the
traditional Gospels, but Jesus is still the main character. So what
about movies like *Star Wars,* The Chronicles of Narnia series, *The
Matrix, The Lion King,* or The Lord of the Rings trilogy? These movies
present stories about good versus evil, the power of redemption, the
importance of remembering your calling, and the temptation of
strength and power. Do these movies have a place in the pulpit and
in our homes? These aren't considered "Christian" movies, nor would
you only find them in the "Religion" section on Netflix, but they too
have an important story to tell.

When the disciples walked with Jesus, "sharing the gospel" was a
matter of physically bringing people to him; however, not long after
his resurrection, Jesus ascended into heaven, leaving the disciples on
earth to continue the ministry and to try to answer the question:
how do you bring people to Jesus when Jesus is no longer "here"?
Forty days or so after his resurrection, Jesus met the disciples on a
mountaintop near Jerusalem. While blessing them, Jesus ascended
into heaven. The disciples were left staring at the sky in awe. Two
men appeared next to them saying, "Men of Galilee, why do you
stand looking up towards heaven? This Jesus, who has been taken

73

u into heaven, will come in the same way as you saw him
eaven" (Acts 1:11 NRSV). This marked a great change in
rch, namely Jesus' absence. The disciples now had to figure
out what following Jesus looked like when there was no Jesus to
physically follow. Of course, Jesus, being the timeless Word of God,
is never absent, but Jesus "in-the-flesh" was no longer there to offer
parables or miracles or healings or hope. This was the moment when
disciples (students) became apostles (sent forth), when followers
became leaders.

So how do you lead people to Jesus when there is no Jesus to see?
There is a difference between talking about Jesus and experiencing
him. Sometimes Jesus talked about himself as the "Son of Man,"
using language like, "I am the light of the world" (John 8:12) in
order to share who God is, but Jesus also told parables about God's
lifesaving grace without mentioning "Messiah," or "Christ," or
"God." Think about the song "Amazing Grace." This hymn is a
powerful witness to the grace God offers through Jesus, but nowhere
in the song is Jesus mentioned. The hymn isn't about Jesus—it is
about experiencing Christ through grace, salvation, being found, and
being a light for generations to come. Another way to think about
this is when Jesus appears to Thomas after the resurrection. Thomas
says that he will not believe that Jesus had been raised unless he
touches Jesus' crucifixion wounds. Jesus appears to him, shows him
his wounds, and says, "Have you believed because you have seen me?
Blessed are those who have not seen and yet have come to believe"
(John 20:29 NRSV). In other words, none of us have walked with
the flesh and blood Jesus from Nazareth, but we are called to have a
deep and abiding relationship with Christ, the timeless and eternal
Word of God.

I have the great blessing of being able to work with an amazing worship band at my local church, The Well. The band is so good, our unofficial slogan is, "The Well United Methodist Church—Where the Music Is Great and the Preaching Tolerable." It is quite liberating as a pastor to work with a talented band or music ensemble because it allows us to really push the boundary of what church music can be. One year, during the season of Lent, we hosted a worship series titled "Jesus Who?" where we shared Jesus' life story through the music of The Who. I will admit that it took some convincing, but when you read the lyrics of the song, "I'm Free," from the musical *Tommy*, it is easy to hear how the gospel message is woven into what most would consider to be secular music: "Messiah's pointed to the door / And no one had the guts to leave the Temple."[2]

Even though The Who aren't singing about Jesus reading from the scroll of Isaiah in Luke 4, this song tells the same story. Jesus said,

> The Spirit of the Lord is upon me,
>> because the Lord has anointed me.
> He has sent me to preach good news to the poor,
>> to proclaim release to the prisoners
>> and recovery of sight to the blind,
>> to liberate the oppressed,
>> and to proclaim the year of the Lord's favor.
>> (Luke 4:18–19)

Jesus rolled up the scroll and told the congregation that this Scripture had been fulfilled in their hearing. They wanted to throw him off a cliff once he revealed that the Messiah had come to those who were outside of the Jewish community! In other words, Jesus said that the Messiah is about good news for those in poverty, liberation for those imprisoned and those blinded by oppression. Jesus pointed to the kingdom, and rather than follow Jesus on his mission, the community didn't have "the guts to leave the Temple." Jesus' message did not fit their expectation of what they thought the Messiah should be. In general, the Jewish tradition expected a Messiah who would establish King David's old kingdom. They hoped that the Messiah would be a military leader and king who would unite an independent nation under the authority of the Temple. Jesus did not meet their expectations.

LOOK TO THE STARS

When Mufasa explains to Simba in *The Lion King* that former kings live up among the stars, the constellation of Leo is visible in the scene's sky.

You may be skeptical that secular movies have much to offer in sharing the gospel, and that's okay. The point is the line between the sacred and the secular might be thinner than we think. I wouldn't necessarily consider *The Lion King* to be a sacred work, until I watch Simba see his deceased father in the clouds, saying, "You have forgotten who you are and therefore have forgotten me," encouraging him to face his past and take his place as rightful king. This would be missed if we only watched movies with "Jesus" in the title. (Never mind the fact that *The Lion King* will probably hold a greater influence on my children than will *Jesus of Nazareth*.) Or how, in *Harry Potter and the Sorcerer's Stone*, Harry wonders why Lord Voldemort cannot touch him. Dumbledore explains that when Harry's mother died while protecting him as a boy, she gifted him with a mark of love. Voldemort was not powerful enough to withstand this powerful seal. I could read Song of Songs to my children—

Set me as a seal over your heart,
   as a seal upon your arm,
for love is as strong as death,
passionate love unrelenting as the grave.
                  (Song of Songs 8:6)

but the closing scene of *Harry Potter* says this in a very memorable and powerful way.

The Letter to the Colossians says, "Through him God was pleased to reconcile to himself all things, whether on earth or in heaven, by making peace through the blood of his cross" (Colossians 1:20 NRSV). God has reconciled all things through Christ, which means that Christ's story of redemption, grace, mercy, and love might be found in the least likely of places—if we are willing to see it!

How would you describe the difference between Jesus and Christ?

Before reading on, what is a movie that doesn't include Jesus that you think expresses the gospel message?

Colossians 1:20 says that God has reconciled all things through Christ. How do you understand the word all *in this verse?*

A LONG TIME AGO, IN A VILLAGE FAR, FAR AWAY

Lord, show us the Father; that will be enough for us.
                        – John 14:8

"A long time ago, in a galaxy far, far away," is a phrase that still makes me hold my breath as I wait for the great orchestral strike that introduces the famous yellow-texted scrolling *Star Wars* title sequence. *Star Wars*, first released in 1977, is the first of many films detailing the epic good-verses-evil struggle between the Galactic Empire and the Rebel Alliance. It's almost silly to detail here what *Star Wars* is about, since almost everyone I've ever met has seen the movie. In fact, I'd bet more young adults can name the five most referenced planets in the *Star Wars* franchise[3] than can name at least five cities that Jesus visited during his ministry.[4] Nevertheless, the first six *Star Wars* movies are about how the Skywalker family brought balance to a mysterious power called the Force.

There are lots of ways to see our Hollywood Jesus in these films. Some would argue that Anakin's virgin birth and powerful connection with the Force is an image of Christ. Others would argue that Luke Skywalker is the obvious Christ figure in the way he resists violence and redeems his father. Maybe Yoda's sought-after wisdom and teachings are the best picture of what it means to seek Christ? Or could it be that Obi-Wan Kenobi best represents the gospel message? At the end of *Star Wars: Episode IV* (sometimes called *A New Hope*) Obi-Wan disappears and becomes "one with the Force" in order to guide Luke in destroying evil, which sounds a lot like when Jesus ascended, telling the disciples that the Holy Spirit would guide them in changing the world. But that's a bit obvious for our Hollywood Jesus. I would argue that the most interesting picture of what it means to be a Christian is found in the person of Han Solo. Allow me to explain from the beginning.

In the *Star Wars: Episode I – The Phantom Menace,* the first of six episodes, we meet Anakin Skywalker, a young boy living on the planet Tatooine. Early in the movie we discover that Anakin doesn't have a father because the Midichlorian, an organic compound found in every living cell, which is the foundation of the Force, conceived him in his mother's womb. In essence, Anakin is the son of a virgin birth (though this isn't explicit). Anakin's mysterious birth and powerful connection with the Force lead the Jedi Council, the governing body of those who follow the light side of the Force, into believing that Anakin is the fulfillment of a prophecy that says that there will one day be balance in both the light and dark sides of the Force. By the end of the third episode, *Revenge of the Sith*, the prophecy holds true. Anakin, now known as the terrible Darth Vader, turns to the dark side of the Force; and by the time the credits roll, there are two Jedi (the light) and two Sith (the dark).

HAVE A LITTLE FAITH, GEORGE

George Lucas, the creator of *Star Wars*, was so convinced that the film was going to fail in the theaters that instead of attending the movie's premiere, he vacationed in Hawaii with his good friend Steven Spielberg, where they came up with the idea for *Raiders of the Lost Ark*.

Episodes four, five, and six of the saga are about Darth Vader's children, Luke and his twin sister. Most of the story revolves around Luke Skywalker leading the rebel alliance to defeat the Galactic Empire. In *A New Hope*, Luke, with the guidance of the Force and Obi-Wan Kenobi, destroys the empire's secret weapon, the Death Star. In episode five, *The Empire Strikes Back*, the empire, well, strikes back and scatters the rebels across the galaxy. Though tempted to join the dark side with his father, Darth Vader, Luke saves the day yet again by refusing to fight his father and give in to his anger. With Luke's refusal to fight, the Emperor has lost in converting Luke to the dark side. The Emperor tries to kill Luke, but before he succeeds, Darth Vader hurls the Emperor into an abyss, saving the day. Does this mean that Anakin once again brought balance to the Force? Does this mean that the story is ultimately about sacrifice and redemption? Maybe not, because episode six, *Return of the Jedi,* suggests that bringing balance to the Force actually means redeeming evil.

And then there's Han Solo. Near the end of *The Empire Strikes Back,* Princess Leah looks longingly into Han Solo's eyes just as he's about to be frozen in carbonite. Fearing that this may be the last time she sees her lover, she says, "I love you," to which Han replies, "I know." This reply is one of the greatest one-liners in all of American cinema, and it wasn't even in the original script. The original script had Han reciprocating his love with a simple, "I love you too"; but the actor, Harrison Ford, improvised and changed the line because, as he said in an interview years later, "Han Solo wouldn't say 'I love you.'"[5] Harrison Ford didn't say "I love you" because it wasn't in Han Solo's character to say it. Han Solo didn't have time for love. He was the rebel, the tough guy, in it for the glory, so when Leah said, "I love you," he just couldn't say it back.

In John 14, Jesus exhorts a grand farewell narrative in which he prepares his disciples for the future. In this particular scene, Jesus is summing things up.

> Philip said, "Lord, show us the Father, and we will be satisfied." Jesus replied, "Have I been with you all this time, Philip, and yet you still don't know who I am? Anyone who has seen me has seen the Father! So why are you asking me to show him to you? Don't you believe that I am in the Father and the Father is in me? The words I speak are not my own, but my Father who lives in me does his work through me." (vv. 8–10 NLT)

Jesus then promises that God will send an Advocate, a guide, a comforter who will teach them and remind them of Christ (vv. 15–18). We, the church, are heirs of this promise. Now that Christ is no longer here in the body, the Spirit allows the church to be the body of Christ, to go out into the world to continue God's story of justice and mercy and hope and love. The Spirit is here, alive, moving within the church, connecting the faithful with the life, suffering, death, and resurrection of Christ.

Several years ago my dad and I were standing out on the beach early in the morning. I asked him, "How do you know God exists?" He looked out on the water at a flock of seagulls flying about and he said, "I know there is a school of fish out beyond that sandbar. I know this because there is a flock of seagulls hovering above the water. You don't have to see the fish to know that they are there. You don't have to see the depths of the ocean to know what's under the surface." But what if you don't even know what you're supposed to be looking for? One of the ways Scripture talks about the Spirit is as a "fierce wind" (Acts 2:2). You can't see it, but you know it's there because of how the wind affects the things around it. You can't see a breeze, but you can see branches sway. You can't see a gust, but you can see waves crashing onto the shore. Sometimes it is hard to see the Spirit, but God, in God's infinite wisdom, gave the church tools to help the church and the world see the Spirit.

When Jesus ascended, not only did God offer the Holy Spirit to the church and the world but God also provided gifts, like baptism and Holy Communion, to help us see and understand the Spirit. It may be hard to see the Spirit, but baptism is like the trees swaying. Holy Communion is like waves crashing onto the shore, shaping and molding the landscape with each wave. It is the Spirit that calls us forward for baptism. It is the Spirit that calls us from our seats to receive the Communion bread and wine. Being baptized and

ating in Holy Communion and Bible study and prayer and of service in the world—these things begin to work on our sou.. The Spirit begins to shape and mold us, and the world begins to look different. When we start to move with the Holy Spirit, we begin to understand more of God's presence in the world. We begin to recognize what's under the surface, that there's a school of fish just beyond the sand bar. We begin to understand ourselves and how we are God's children. Through the Holy Spirit we begin to understand our true Christian character, that we are the body of Christ and that we are called to say "I love you" to the world.

Which other characters in Star Wars do you think point to the gospel story?

What are some ways you say "I love you" to those you care about?

How would you answer the question, "Does God exist? "What examples would you use?

Put on Your Sunday Clothes

He was pierced because of our rebellions,
and crushed because of our crimes.
He bore the punishment that made us whole;
by his wounds we are healed. – Isaiah 53:5

Sometimes you can say "I love you" without using words. One of the most impressive things about Disney/Pixar's *WALL-E* is how a small robot is able to communicate what it means to love, serve, and bring about life with only the ability to say its own name. In fact, nearly the only words spoken in the first half of the film is a recorded song WALL-E plays in his workshop. The song, "Put on Your Sunday Clothes" from the musical *Hello, Dolly!* should be a clue that the gospel is being shared. No, *WALL-E* isn't about Jesus, but it is about love's beauty, life's importance, and freedom's power.

The movie begins with a dead, deserted planet Earth. There are no signs of life other than a small cockroach scampering about. We see WALL-E, a small trash-compacting robot, performing his prescribed duty of cleaning up the trash that humanity, long since gone, has left behind. WALL-E seems to be the only robot left to do what appears to be a hopeless task, but WALL-E is faithful and curious. He looks at all of the abandoned knickknacks with a sense of awe and wonder, slowly piecing together what humanity is by what they've left behind.

Have you ever wondered what you might leave behind when you're gone? What do your possessions say about the life you live? The images of skyscraper-tall towers of trash in *WALL-E* hit home, don't they? A quick inventory of my junk drawer (full, of course, of all the stuff I might need one day) shows three rather useless cell phone chargers. I guess I could throw them away. I would probably feel better if I did, but seeing the mountains of trash in *WALL-E* reminds me that those useless cell phone chargers end up somewhere—the Environmental Protection Agency reported that Americans generated 251 millions tons of trash in 2012 alone![6]

But the beauty of WALL-E's story goes beyond environmental stewardship. Early in the film, a small scouting probe named EVE (don't miss the symbolism!) is sent to Earth to look for signs of life. After finding a small seedling, EVE, along with a hitchhiking WALL-E, are rocketed back to *Axiom*, a ship that was constructed to save all life on Earth (reminiscent of Noah's ark?). Life certainly looks different on *Axiom* than it did on Earth, though. All of the humans have lost bone and muscle mass while in deep space, which means they have lost the ability to walk. Instead, they ride around in hover chairs with full digital screens in front of their faces in order to communicate and even order their next meal. They don't so much as have to turn their heads to receive anything they want. A single corporation, Buy 'n' Large, controls everything from when the "sun" rises to what kind of fashion is "in," to what kinds of food they eat. It seems as though humanity is just on an endless, mindless cruise vacation, until the audience realizes the corporation is using the ship as a means of controlling humanity.

WHAT'S IN A NAME?

The human transport ship in *WALL-E* is named *Axiom,* which means, "something unquestionable or taken for granted," in logic and mathematics.

It makes me wonder…who and what are we being controlled by? In your life, who is in charge of saying what food is good, which clothes should be worn, what size your house should be, and how you should use your time? Of course we need food, clothing, and shelter, all of which we often take for granted in the United States, but who or what controls the narrative of those things? What voices are we listening to? It's like when the first man and woman, Adam and Eve, were in the Garden of Eden and the snake deceived them (oh yes, the man was there too—read the story in Genesis 3:6). The snake questioned what God had commanded them about eating the fruit of the tree of the knowledge of good and evil: "You will not die; for God knows that when you eat of it your eyes will be opened, and you will be like God, knowing good and evil" (Genesis 3:4–5 NRSV). Thus an idol-worshipping seed was planted in the human heart: wouldn't life be better if we were gods rather than depending on God? The woman sees that the tree is good for food, and a delight

84

to the eyes, and is to be desired for wisdom. What's so wrong with goodness, delight, and desire? Nothing. The problem is that it was the tree that was good and delightful and desired, not the Creator of the tree.

In my city there are three grocery stores on a one-mile stretch of highway. On the one hand, having three stores so close to each other seems to foster healthy competition, which can be a good thing. The only problem is, I only want to go to one store. So if I'm going to the grocery to buy some apples, I'm probably going to buy more than I need either because I don't have time to find the best deal or I might run out and the other stores might be out too. By and large, the abundance of stores actually reinforces my sense of scarcity—I'm still afraid it all won't be enough. The computers on the *Axiom* know this—on the ship, humanity has all that it needs, and yet they still run advertisements of the latest color and the trendiest drink in order to create a sense of scarcity, which drives desire.

WALL-E appears to be immune to this influence, so it isn't long before WALL-E runs into trouble. While searching for EVE, he accidentally knocks a woman from her hover chair. At first she's troubled—she probably hasn't been out of her chair in years. Then she looks up, and seemingly for the first time, she sees the world around her without the aid of the screen. She's mesmerized at what she's been missing—"I didn't know we had a pool!"

By way of accident, WALL-E restores her vision, or he offers "recovery of sight to the blind" (Luke 4:18). Later WALL-E finds himself in a containment unit for faulty robots, where he accidentally destroys the power source that is keeping all the robots confined, or he "[Lets] the oppressed go free" (Luke 4:18 NRSV). After finding EVE, WALL-E takes the plant from Earth and struggles to put it in the heart of the ship, potentially ending humanity's exile in outer space and restoring hope for a new Earth. Buy 'n' Large's power-hungry computer fights back by crushing WALL-E as he is restoring life. Sound familiar?

> Who can believe what we have heard,
>   and for whose sake has the LORD's arm been revealed?
> He grew up like a young plant before us,
>   like a root from dry ground.
> He possessed no splendid form for us to see,
>   no desirable appearance.
> He was despised and avoided by others;
>   a man who suffered, who knew sickness well.
> Like someone from whom people hid their faces,
>   he was despised, and we didn't think about him.
> It was certainly our sickness that he carried,
>   and our sufferings that he bore,
>   but we thought him afflicted,
>   struck down by God and tormented.
> He was pierced because of our rebellions
>   and crushed because of our crimes.
> He bore the punishment that made us whole;
>   by his wounds we are healed. (Isaiah 53:1–5)

Eventually WALL-E is able to deliver the plant into the heart of the *Axiom*, and humanity returns to Earth in order to reseed and repopulate creation. As the camera zooms out on the last scene, we see a hill in the distance on which plants are already growing, revealing that while WALL-E was away and humanity was woefully absent, a creator was already working behind the scenes to bring life to an empty planet. Amen. Through Christ, God surely does supply our every need (see Philippians 4:19).

Do you think WALL-E offers an accurate picture of what the world could be like in the future?

Have you ever had an "I didn't know we had a pool!" moment? What was it about?

In what ways have you noticed God working in the background of your life?

THERE AND BACK AGAIN

The desire to do good is inside of me, but I can't do it. I don't do the good that I want to do, but I do the evil that I don't want to do. – Romans 7:18b–19

A movie doesn't have to mention Jesus in order to share an experience of Christ, just like Jesus' parables reveal who God is without explicitly mentioning God. Sometimes a movie can be an extended metaphor about God's kingdom. C. S. Lewis created the world of Narnia in order to express the magnificence of what he saw God doing in the world, and although J. R. R. Tolkien's epic The Lord of the Rings trilogy wasn't written explicitly to share the gospel, its message certainly reveals the beauty and truth of God's kingdom. And sometimes Scripture—viewed through Christ's suffering, death, and resurrection—takes on new meaning.

"The Binding of Isaac" in Genesis 22 is a difficult story because in it God calls for the faithful Abraham to sacrifice his beloved son, Isaac, on a far-off mountaintop. This story leaves us with troubling questions about God's will, questions we feel compelled to solve but which only birth more questions. This story is like a ballet— the moves are definitive, plié down left, relevé and lift—but the dancers' inner dialogue is left to interpretation. But through patient reading and a keen eye, Scripture's silent movements come together to reveal a beautiful story. This dance between Abraham, Isaac, and God seems to defy ethics and suspend any type of moral rule, but as we look at the larger story, this terrible occasion can point us to the fulfillment of God's promise to Abraham in the person of Christ.

There is little inner dialogue in the story. We don't know what Abraham is thinking. We don't know whether or not Isaac was a willing participant. All we know in terms of inner dialogue, or thought, is that God is testing Abraham, and this is crucial to the story. It's like when you hear that awful screeching sound on the radio and then a soothing voice says, "This is a test. This is only a test." It's as if the author of this story wants us to know that this is not a story condoning child abuse. Abraham is being tested in this situation, not commanded as he was when God said, "Leave your land, your family, and your father's household for the land that I will show you" (Genesis 12:1) even though the language in this story is very similar—"Take your son, your only son whom you love, Isaac, and go to the land of Moriah. Offer him up as an entirely burned offering there on one of the mountains that I will show you" (Genesis 22:2) Go, Abraham. Go, and leave your family behind.

The obedient Abraham rose early in the morning and set out with Isaac and two other servants. While on the journey, Abraham and Isaac have their only recorded conversation in the Bible. Isaac said, "Father," and again Abraham says, "Here I am." "The fire and the wood are here, but where is the lamb for a burnt offering?" Abraham replies, "God himself will provide the lamb for a burnt offering, my son." Abraham's response exemplifies the ambiguity of the story. This statement can be understood in two completely different ways. The first, "God himself will provide the lamb, my son," seems to suggest that Abraham trusted that God was not going to allow this sacrifice to take place. The other way of hearing this statement, "God himself will provide the lamb—my son," suggests that God promised Isaac for the sole purpose of this sacrifice. In this reading it sounds as though Abraham is fully expecting to sacrifice his son. What is Abraham thinking? We don't know, and I'm not sure that we are supposed to.

On the third day they finally reach their destination on Mount Moriah, which coincidentally (maybe) is the same place the fellowship lose their way in Tolkien's *The Fellowship of the Ring*. While traveling through the Mines of Moriah (an interesting play on mountain versus mine) the pathway through the mountain becomes forked, and Gandalf can't remember which way to go. This fellowship—a group comprised of humans, hobbits, a wizard, a dwarf, and an elf—have been given the task of destroying the Ring of Power created by the evil Lord Sauron. The task is simple. All they have to do is throw the ring into the fires of Mount Doom, forever destroying evil, but the making of the journey to the mountain is a nearly impossible feat. Being a follower of Jesus is pretty simple: love God and love your neighbor, though the journey takes a lifetime to master. It is an impossible journey without God's help, or as Jesus said, "What is impossible for humans is possible for God" (Luke 18:27). While the fellowship considers which way to go, Frodo, the ring-bearer, mentions to the wizard Gandalf that he wished the ring had never come to him, that he didn't have to carry the burden of it all. Gandalf replies:

> So do all who live to see such times. But that is not for them to decide. All we have to decide is what to do with the time that is given to us. There are other forces at work in this world, Frodo, besides the will of evil. Bilbo was meant

to find the Ring. In which case, you were also meant to have it. And that is an encouraging thought.[7]

Interestingly, after Gandalf offers the hope of a greater power at work, he suddenly remembers which way to go.

After Abraham climbs Mount Moriah, he binds the hands and feet of his son, Isaac, preparing to sacrifice his son as the Lord has commanded. But as Abraham's knife is coming down to offer the sacrifice, a messenger of the Lord swoops in and tells Abraham not to harm the boy. God then says, "Now I know that you fear God because you have not withheld your son from me." *Now I know*, says God. Was this a test of Abraham's faith in God, or was God testing his own divine faith in establishing a covenant with humanity? In other words, maybe this story is not about if Abraham would follow through with God's request or not, but whether or not God was willing and patient enough to be our God.

That is why I love movies like *The Fellowship of the Ring*—because they offer us the space to ask questions that we sometimes feel shy about asking when we read Scripture. The Lord of the Rings trilogy isn't about Jesus, but it is about the power of sin and the false promise sin offers. Fundamentally, the Ring of Power symbolizes the power of addiction. Whoever carries the ring is offered power and strength, but over time he begins to lose his identity and the ring begins to control his actions. It's like when Paul talks about sin in Romans 7:

> I don't know what I'm doing, because I don't do what I want to do. Instead, I do the thing that I hate. But if I'm doing the thing that I don't want to do, I'm agreeing that the Law is right. But now I'm not the one doing it anymore. Instead, it's sin that lives in me. I know that good doesn't live in me--that is, in my body. The desire to do good is inside of

me, but I can't do it. I don't do the good that I want to do, but I do the evil that I don't want to do. But if I do the very thing that I don't want to do, then I'm not the one doing it anymore. Instead, it is sin that lives in me that is doing it.

(Romans 7:15–20)

All they have to do is journey to Mount Doom and throw the ring into the fire. At the end, Frodo finally makes it to the edge of the furnace, and you can see that the impossible mission is almost over. He holds the ring over the fire, but then pauses, brings it back, holds it close to his chest, and says, "It's mine!" Addiction is powerful indeed. All you have to do is put down the bottle, throw the cigarettes away, and walk away from the cookies, but it just isn't that easy, is it? One of my friends and colleagues pokes fun at The Lord of the Rings trilogy (in his quest to show that *Star Wars* is the more appropriate vision of God's kingdom, bless his heart) because most of the books contain thousands of words dedicated to just walking somewhere. The fellowship walks here and there, back and forth, up the mountains and back down again. In fact, the subtitle of the prequel to the story, *The Hobbit*, is *There and Back Again*. But that's kind of the point, isn't it? It's about the journey. It's about walking with Christ. It's not about getting into heaven—it's about the discipleship walk with Christ so that we will recognize the gift of heaven that's already been given to us.

SPEAKING THE LANGUAGE

Much of the Elvish language spoken in The Lord of the Rings films was derived from J. R. R. Tolkien's own limited dictionary of the Elvish language, which he created for use in his fiction.

The story of the binding of Isaac is a long and difficult story (some might say the same about The Lord of the Rings). The story actually spans thousands of years, and ends with Jesus. Isaac's question, "Where is the lamb?" has been answered." "The Lord will provide the lamb, my son." The son, Christ Jesus, is the lamb for the world. Through Christ's suffering, death, and resurrection, we have found life. We have become heirs of Abraham's promise, a promise that allows us to see the story of Christ in the most terrible and inexplicable situations. Neither The Lord of the Rings nor Abraham's story is about Jesus, but they each tell Christ's story, a story about how resurrection has now conquered the power of sin and death. "Where is your victory, death? Where is your sting?" (1 Corinthians 15:55).

If you were to name it, what is "the ring" in your life? What do you find difficult to let go?

Do you agree that all we have to decide is, as Gandalf says, "what to do with the time given to us"? Why or why not?

How would you describe your walk with Christ? Is it long and difficult? Is it fast and on the move? Do you just feel like you're going there and back again?

REMEMBER WHO YOU ARE

You are my Son, whom I dearly love; in you I find happiness. – Luke 3:22b

After Jesus ascended, the disciples had to work with the Holy Spirit in order to figure out what walking with Christ looked like when Jesus was no longer present. Jesus was gone, but by the power of the Holy Spirit, Christ's presence lives within everyone who believes. God did not leave us orphaned (John 14:18). God offered us the sacraments, the holy gifts of baptism and Holy Communion, to be buoys for us in the stormy sea of life. In *The Fellowship of the Ring*, just before Frodo sets out to destroy the ring of power, he is offered a coat of *mithril* (a lightweight but very durable Elven thread) to cover him against attack, and a dagger, named *Sting*, to ward off enemies. Yes, our journeys too are long and difficult at times, but God offers us gifts (sacraments) along the way to aid and protect us, and Hollywood Jesus offers us a language to help communicate baptism's gift and Holy Communion's beauty.

My children love *The Lion King*. Midway through the movie, there is a great scene that talks about forgiveness, redemption, and the calling to ministry we have all received through our baptism in Christ, but if I described that, in that language, to my five-year-old, it wouldn't be nearly as memorable as when Simba looks into the clouds and hears Mufasa say, "Remember who you are."

The movie's drama escalates when Mufasa, the king of the lions, is killed. His son, Simba, blames himself for Mufasa's death and runs off, exiling himself to the wilderness outside of the African pride lands. Simba's uncle, Scar, assumes the throne, abusing both the land and the animals for personal gain. Rafiki, a wise baboon mystic of sorts, reads the changing of the wind and discovers that Simba is alive. He journeys into the wilderness to convince Simba to return and take his place in the great circle of life as king, but Simba is skeptical, having spent years racked with grief and shame. Rafiki leads him to the water's edge, and Simba looks into the pool and sees his own reflection; but after Rafiki tells him to "look harder" into the water, Simba sees his father's face is staring back at him. Mufasa's image then appears in the clouds, saying, "You have forgotten who you are and have so forgotten me...you are more than what you have become...remember who you are. You are my son and the one true king. Remember who you are."[8] Simba is afraid to face his past, but wise Rafiki says that the past can hurt, but that one can either run from it, or learn from it. Simba, noticing that the wind is changing, runs back to the pride lands in order to redeem the past.

Baptism is a sign of what God has done, is doing, and will do in our lives. Baptism washes us of our sin and welcomes us into Christ's life expressed through the church. It is a gift that moves toward us before we move toward God. God prepares the waters for baptism even before we show up to get dunked! Baptism is a gift that unites us to the life, suffering, death, and resurrection of Christ. It is a gift of the Holy Spirit that walks with us each and every day, calling us to remember that we are God's children, heirs to God's promise in the great circle of everlasting life, which begins and ends with God.

Baptism is also a means of forgiveness for sin. When you come forward for baptism in my church, we ask three questions. The first is: "Do you renounce the spiritual forces of wickedness, reject the evil powers of the world, and repent of your sin?" In other words, are you ready to turn around and start living into God's will for your life? Next we ask, "Do you accept the freedom and power God gives you to resist evil, injustice, and oppression, in whatever forms they present themselves?" To resist evil simply means to redefine what is good. I don't think that offering a list of sins to avoid is helpful. When I was a youth director, before a lock-in I would sit the youth down and give them the rules. I would say things like, "Don't go outside the building at night," and "When the lights are out, it's time to go to sleep." These are certainly helpful, but my exhaustive list continued with things like, "Don't make out with your significant other in the stairwell at 3:00 in the morning," and "Don't sneak vodka in your water bottle." I quickly discovered that this list of "don'ts" was nothing more than a brainstorming opportunity for my kids. It just gave them ideas about what they *couldn't* do. A much better way to live into being a Christian is to highlight the good and redefine what good is. A great question to ask is, "Are your decisions life-giving?" because sin doesn't give life. Or, "Is what I am doing harmful?" because sin always is.

The last question we ask those about to be baptized is, "Do you confess Jesus Christ as your Savior and put your whole trust in his grace?" In other words, you don't have to do this alone! In fact, you *can't*. I love the question, "Do you trust in the grace?" Do you trust solely in the grace and forgiveness and love of Jesus Christ? Do you trust that Christ will keep his promise? That's a much different question than, "Do you promise never to screw up?"

In the church we often talk about remembering your baptism. We say, "Remember your baptism and be thankful." I was baptized as an infant, so I don't remember my baptism. I have to rely on community for the remembrance of my baptism. What a great reminder that we aren't alone in this journey! When we say, "Remember your baptism," we mean to remember and claim that you are a beloved child of God. Remember to turn around and walk where Christ is leading. Remember that it is not money or fame or power, but it is God who is our definition of good. Remember that, in good days or bad, for richer for poorer, in sickness and in health, to trust that Jesus loves you.

Baptism isn't the only gift that God has offered you. Holy Communion is a reminder that you are always welcome to God's table, that no matter where you are on your faith journey, you are always called to remember Christ and reconnect with Christ's life-giving grace. Disney/Pixar's film *Ratatouille* is a movie about an ordinary rat who loves to cook and who decides to pursue that dream. In one of my favorite scenes, a food critic—Anton Ego, a cold, frail, no-nonsense kind of guy—comes into the restaurant, and of all the dishes they could serve, the rat decides to make ratatouille, a French peasant's dish. It's as if your boss came over for dinner, and you decided to whip up Ramen noodles or Kraft Macaroni & Cheese, both of which I am very familiar with. Rejecting the advice from his colleagues, the rat dishes up the ratatouille, and when Ego takes a bite of the dish, his mind immediately harkens back to his boyhood home kitchen table where his mom comforts him with a warm bowl of ratatouille. The cold critic drops his pen, symbolizing the laying down of his pretention and self-importance. His life is forever changed by the meal.

When Jesus ascended to heaven, it was up to the disciples to figure out the path ahead with the guidance of the Holy Spirit. And though we never physically walked with Jesus, we believers still feel his absence here on Earth and long for the day we will be reunited with him. But we are not alone. God has given us many gifts to help us remember that we are his beloved children—baptism and Holy Communion, along with study, fellowship, service, and prayer—and to accompany us along the fantastic journey we call life. And through even the medium of film we can remember that truth as well. We can remember this profound truth when Simba looks into the sky or when Anton Ego has a life-changing meal. We can remember Christ's sacrifice through watching a little robot offer new life to the world, and feel Christ's victory over death when an evil ring is finally destroyed. Even when Jesus isn't with us on Earth, or before us on the screen, the gospel is still active and present. May we have eyes to see it.

Have you ever been baptized? If so, in what ways do you remember your baptism?

How is Holy Communion celebrated in your faith community? Who is welcome to the table?

What other gifts has God offered you for your life's journey? How have you accepted those gifts?

Chapter Four

EVERYONE HAS A STORY

I have been crucified with Christ and I no longer live, but
Christ lives in me. And the life that I now live in my body,
I live by faith, indeed, by the faithfulness of God's Son,
who loved me and gave himself for me.

— Galatians 2:20

As a child, I imagined that the world around me was created just for me. It's not that I thought I was the center of the universe and the most important thing in it (others might disagree), but it seemed that someone had gone through a lot of trouble to create a very elaborate world and had put me in it, so I couldn't help but wonder, *What's my role in all this?*

I remember seeing *The Truman Show* and thinking, *Someone finally understands!* The movie is about man named Truman Burbank, and the world that has been created around him since his birth. Living in an idyllic town, full of polite and caring people, Truman thinks he has a great life. But what he doesn't know is that he is actually the star of his own television show—that his entire life has been a secretly taped reality television program, masterminded by a "creator" who built an elaborate world for Truman to live in. Everyone in his life is a paid actor. His town is a purposefully build stage set surrounded by a massive dome. Even the sun, moon, and horizon have been created to perpetuate the illusion of reality. Truman is blissfully unaware that people in the real world are voyeuristically watching him live out his daily life, until one day a strange object—a studio light—falls out of the "sky," and Truman's world begins to unravel as the questions come flooding in. At the end of the film, in a scene representing death and rebirth, Truman sails a boat to the horizon, reaches the end of the dome, and finds a set of stairs leading to a door. He walks through the door, and thus dares to his place in a new world.

PSALM 139

In *The Truman Show,* Truman's boat has "139" displayed on its sail, a subtle nod to Psalm 139, which is referenced several times throughout the film.

God created each and every one of us—his children—and gave us a place in this world so that we all might learn to love God and love each other. So far we have been discussing movies about Jesus and movies about the gospel message, but now I want to shift the focus to include how each of our stories plays a part in God's story. For me, it can be helpful to see a movie about Jesus in order to learn more about the gospel story, but because the story happened two thousand years ago, it can be difficult to find my place in that story. Likewise, seeing movies about Christ figures helps us understand resurrection, love, mercy, and grace, but I have to face the fact that I will never be Superman or Frodo or WALL-E. That's why I love movies like *Cool Hand Luke, One Flew Over the Cuckoo's Nest,* and *Jesus of Montreal*— they are stories about regular people doing extraordinary things, and they remind us that regular people like you and me have a very important role to play in sharing God's love with a broken world. I will never have Luke Skywalker's lightsaber, but I can have a cool hand like Luke Jackson.

WHAT'S MISSING?

At this point you may be screaming at the book saying something like, "Why haven't you mentioned [insert movie here]?" or "How could he miss that [insert movie here] is the best example of what it means to be a Christian?" or "He only spent three sentences on the Harry Potter franchise? What a joke!" Fair enough. There's not enough space to cover every Hollywood Jesus that's out there, but the movies missing from this book aren't what we should be concerned about. What is troubling is what's missing in the theaters—that most of the movies we've discussed are about men. It is true that Jesus was a man working within a patriarchal society. It's reasonable that films about Jesus reflect first-century Palestinian culture, but why couldn't Mufasa and Sarabi have a daughter who assumed the throne of Pride Rock? Why couldn't Trinity be the chosen one in *The Matrix*? You could argue that even though WALL-E and EVE are robots, they both seem to embody male and female characteristics, and the more "male" character of WALL-E ends up saving the day. Not only is Hollywood Jesus mostly male, but people of color are tragically underrepresented too.

We are *all*—every race, male and female—called to live out the gospel. Hollywood Jesus has some room for growth in representing all of God's children. Maybe you are the one to bring about change to our Hollywood Jesus? Maybe in reading this book you are being called to offer us a new picture of what it means to be a follower of Jesus Christ. Maybe it's time for you to pick up the camera and show us how you understand Jesus in your context and community. Maybe what's missing is you.

Sometimes Nothing Can Be a Real Cool Hand

When God began to create the heavens and the earth—
the earth was without shape or form, it was dark over the
deep sea, and God's wind swept over the waters.
                                            – Genesis 1:1–2

To create something out of nothing is typically reserved only for God. Many talk about creation as *creation ex nihilo*, meaning that God brought forth creation, not by combining elements of what was already there, but out of nothing at all. It's like the story about the scientist who told God that he no longer needed God in order to create life. God gave his blessing to the scientist to create life. The scientist began to gather together what he needed to create life in the laboratory. God stopped him and said, "Get your own ingredients."

Creating something out of what seems to be nothing is an important Christian discipline. The best example of creating something out of what seems to be nothing is the Hollywood Jesus found in the person of Luke Jackson. *Cool Hand Luke* (1967) is the story about a regular guy, Luke Jackson, who gets arrested for cutting off the tops of parking meters. Almost immediately after going to jail, it's easy to tell that Luke is a bit different from the other prisoners. He seems to be above the fray and not easily influenced by the hierarchy that exists behind the barbed-wire fence.

Early in the movie, Dragline, the boisterous prisoner ringleader, challenges Luke to a Saturday morning fistfight. At the beginning of the fight, the men cheer for Dragline, hoping that he might teach this new inmate a lesson. Rather than fighting back, Luke stands in the dirt-filled ring and just takes punches, one after the other, rarely throwing a punch himself. Dragline keeps beating him to the point where the violence makes the onlookers squeamish. The spectators eventually stop watching the fight, turned off by the beating Luke receives. Instead of resisting the fight or winning the fight, Luke chooses to turn the other cheek, and so ends the practice of Saturday morning fistfights. Nonviolence won. Through resisting rather than being on the offensive, Luke wins the respect of the other prisoners and ends the practice of backyard fighting. The other prisoners no longer seem interested in working out their problems through punches. This may be an extreme example of what Jesus meant when he said, "Turn the other cheek" (see Luke 6:29), but it is a great example of how to win a fight.

GETTING THE JOB DONE
In the "road-tarring" sequence of *Cool Hand Luke*, the actors who played prisoners actually blacktopped a mile-long stretch of highway.

Later in the movie Luke is playing poker with the rest of the guys, and he keeps raising and raising and raising the pot. It's as if he doesn't even care about the few dollars he has. At the end of the game, when the cards are finally revealed, the guys see that he had nothing in his hand. Dragline says, "He beat you with nothing. Just like today when he kept coming back at me…with nothing!" Luke simply replies, "Yeah, well…Sometimes nothing can be a real cool hand."[1]

Violence and sin and the lust for money are really nothing—they are the formless void that God saw upon the earth when he began to create. Maybe that's what Jesus means when he talks about turning the other cheek and "You cannot serve God and wealth" (Matthew 6:24). Then God created something out of that nothing. By resisting violence, by not allowing money and power to rule over us, we reenact the divine action of creating something out of nothing. It's like in John 6, when thousands of people were following Jesus and they had nothing to eat. Jesus asked the disciples to feed the crowd, but Andrew said, "There is a boy here who has five barley loaves and two fish. But what are they among so many people?" In other words, the disciples thought they had nothing. Jesus took their "nothing" and fed thousands with it. God is doing it again—making something out of nothing!

One of my friends in ministry shared with me the blessings and woes of working with his congregation's missions committee. Their annual budget for missions was $500, and the missions committee always saw this as a defeat. They assumed that there wasn't much they could do to serve the kingdom, yet they went ahead with the normal seasonal missions. For Thanksgiving they cooked a meal for those who were hungry. They collected toys for children in the area for Christmas. They bought plastic eggs and candy for the neighborhood Easter egg hunt. They were faithful with what they had. Then one day someone willed the committee $1,500 upon her passing, so the next year they had $2,000 in the mission account. Now the sky was the limit for this community, and they started brainstorming as to how they could use the money. They decided to collect food for the food bank, so each member went to the store and gathered an extra item or two, and they donated several hundred pounds of food. Later they decided to write get-well cards to people in the hospital. They also decided to go out into the neighborhood and pick up trash that lined the streets and ditches. For Easter they decided to have a special worship service where they would gather and play all the old favorite hymns about triumph and glory. They offered some pretty remarkable things to their community. At the end of the year, the committee experienced an interesting miracle—they discovered that there was still $2,000 in the account. They had made something out of what they thought was nothing.

Sometimes we take God's gifts for granted, thinking that if we only had a little more we could really accomplish what God is calling us to accomplish in the world. But when we turn our hearts to see the abundant gifts God has already offered us through Christ, we quickly realize God has already equipped us to change the world. Maybe God did create *ex nihilo*, creating something out of nothing. And maybe that is precisely what he is calling us to do in the world. Saint Francis wrote:

> Lord, make me an instrument of your peace;
> where there is hatred, let me sow love;
> where there is injury, pardon;
> where there is doubt, faith;
> where there is despair, hope;
> where there is darkness, light;
> and where there is sadness, joy.[2]

Or in other words, where there is nothing, Lord help me create something.

What might creating something out of nothing look like in your faith community?

What are some gifts you can offer to God so that God might multiply them for the kingdom?

In what ways can a commitment to nonviolence bring peace to your community?

PLASTIC JESUS

"Well, I don't care if it rains or freezes, / Long as I have my plastic Jesus."[3]

But wait—we aren't finished with *Cool Hand Luke* just yet. The task set before us is not just about creating something out of nothing—the something we create should reflect the love, mercy, grace, and abundance of God's kingdom. There's a scene in the movie where Luke makes a bet that he can eat fifty hard-boiled eggs. Dragline is quick to ask Luke, "You ever eat fifty eggs? Luke simply replies, "Nobody ever eat fifty eggs." The prisoners give Luke an hour to accomplish the impossible, and sure enough, Luke eats the fifty eggs. After accomplishing this amazing feat, he lies on a table in cruciform like Jesus on the cross. A prisoner walks by and says under his breath, "No man can eat fifty eggs." This reminds me of Jesus' miracle of feeding the multitudes in Matthew 14. Jesus took what the disciples thought was nothing and fed the crowds with leftover fish and bread. The disciples basically said, "No man can feed five thousand people with five loaves and two fish." Jesus accomplishes what was thought to be impossible, and he leaves the crowd in awe over God's abundance.

One day Jesus met a wealthy man who thought he had everything. He asked Jesus, "What good thing must I do to have eternal life?" (Matthew 19:16), as if eternal life was another possession the man could purchase. Jesus told the man that if he was looking for something to do, then he should keep the commandments. The man answered that he had already kept them, to which Jesus replied, "If you want to be complete, go, sell what you own, and give the money to the poor. Then you will have treasure in heaven. And come follow me" (Matthew 19:21). The man walked away in sorrow because he was very rich, and apparently he didn't want that to change. Often, when the something that God offers for our nothing is too great for our imagination, we just walk away, thinking that following God is impossible, or at least outside of our limited ability.

After the man left, Jesus looked to the disciples and said, "I assure you that it will be very hard for a rich person to enter the kingdom of heaven. In fact, it's easier for a camel to squeeze through the eye of a needle than for a rich person to enter God's kingdom" (Matthew 19:23-24). If feeding the multitudes left the disciples in awe, this teaching left them perplexed. You can almost hear them thinking, *We have a problem here... if the goal is for a camel to go through the eye of a needle, then we either need an extremely small camel or a too-large-to-be-functional needle.* Let's explore option number one—the camel is much too large for the needle.

In *Alice in Wonderland,* Alice follows the Rabbit through the rabbit hole to a world of wonder and absurdity, which is not unlike our Christian journey. She comes to a door and tries to follow the Rabbit, but the doorknob says to her, "You cannot fit through. You are much too big. Simply impassible."

To which Alice replies, "You mean impossible."

"No, impassible," says the doorknob. "Nothing's impossible."

Whether we like it or not, this camel-needle story is about our love affair with money. We squirm in our seats when people talk about money because we're in love with it, as was the rich young ruler who approached Jesus. What Jesus was saying to him was, "You are carrying too much to follow me. You, Mr. Camel, are much too big."

Go, sell all that is yours, and give the money to the poor. What simple and difficult words. I think we are all biblical literalists until we get to verses like these. Granted, it is curious advice. If someone is in need of food, and you sell your food and give them money to buy food, the only person enjoying this plan is the shop owner. It seems rather capitalistic of Jesus, to be frank. Wouldn't you expect Jesus to say, "Give what you own to the poor"? Wouldn't that make it easier? We can use our own reasoning to do what we think best, but as the residents of Wonderland quickly learned, if the Queen of Hearts wants red roses, don't plant white roses and paint them red—just plant red roses.

If Jesus says sell all you own and give the money to the poor, he has his reasons. Consider this scenario: Imagine if your boss, instead of handing you a check, gave you the TV she doesn't use anymore or the suit he's outgrown, or instead of paying you, he gives you a coupon for a list of groceries he has purchased for you. Would you feel valued by him or her? Sometimes giving to the poor can be demeaning for the recipients. Several years ago I went on a mission trip to New York City, specifically to help at the St. Andrews/ St. Paul's Food Pantry. They had quite a remarkable system. Each item on the shelves had a point allotted to it, so I asked the lady behind the desk what the point system was about. She said that the poor in the neighborhood earn points according to the kind and amount of service they give to the community, and they can then use the points for items in the store. This provides much more dignity and empowerment to those in need, instead of being given the hand-me-downs of the wealthy. So, "go, sell all that you own and give the money to the poor" makes perfect sense, because in doing so, you are empowering the poor and your hands are free and open to embrace God's gifts of eternal life.

On the other hand, selling all that you own can seem like the Dodo's caucus race by the sea, where everyone is running around in an endless race. If the man sells everything he owns, then he becomes precisely who he is trying to help. This seems rather pointless until we realize that this is exactly what God has done in the person of

Jesus. God emptied himself, put on flesh, and was born under the Law so that God might fulfill the Law and bring about the kingdom in which we find eternal life. Saint Athanasius is rumored to have said that God cannot redeem what God did not assume, which is why God put on flesh and walked among us. In other words, God had to become human in order to save humanity. Those who love money—that is, those who love the goods from God more than God's goodness—are much too big to enter into the kingdom. The camel must be smaller. We must empty ourselves, as Christ emptied himself.

During a rainstorm, Luke, in defiant confidence, shouts up to heaven for God to take his life. He calls out for God to show him a sign that he is there. Then he shrugs the moment off, saying, "I'm just standing in the rain talking to myself." Later that night Luke receives a telegram saying that his mother has died. It's a curious moment. Is this an answer to Luke's request for a sign? Regardless, he picks up his banjo in a moment of Jonah-like mockery and sings, "Well, I don't care if it rains or freezes, / Long as I have my plastic Jesus."[4]

Sometimes nothing isn't such a cool hand, especially when we think that the "nothing" we have is from God. God's promise was never that we would be safe from harm or that we would never know pain or grief—God's promise is to always be with us in those moments of sadness, as well as in moments of joy. Luke repeats the second part of the song with a strange and somber assurance, reminiscent of Jesus' plea in the garden, "My Father, if it is possible, let this cup pass from me; yet not what I want but what you want" (Matthew 26:39 NRSV). It seems as though the something Luke has found in the midst of nothing is nothing but sorrow. Throughout the movie Luke lives in perpetual "Garden of Gethsemane" moment. He calls out to God over and again with no answer from heaven, and yet he continues to offer joy, hope, and something out of nothing. In his own way he too is saying, "Let this cup pass from me; yet not what I want but what you want."

Sometimes the idea that Jesus has conquered all can feel "plastic" or empty when we are in the midst of experiencing suffering, pain, and hardship. There have been times in my life when God has been silent, and I was certainly troubled when my frustrated prayers were met with silence. But one day I realized that the silence I experience is actually what it sounds like when God is listening. In the book of Job, Job experiences great loss and consuming despair, and his friends surround him to share in his grief—"They sat with Job on the ground seven days and seven nights, not speaking a word to him, for they saw that he was in excruciating pain" (Job 2:13). Like Job's friends, even when God is silent, his presence is with us, sharing our grief and sadness. But God's silence doesn't last long. After listening to our soul, that is when God, through Christ, speaks words of redemption, forgiveness, pardon, and grace.

What kind of hand do you think you've been given? What about your friends? What about your enemies?

Poverty is a complex issue. What's one thing you and your faith community can do to break the cycle of poverty in your town?

TAKING THE RED PILL

You take the blue pill, the story ends. You wake up in your bed and believe whatever you want to believe. You take the red pill, you stay in Wonderland, and I show you how deep the rabbit hole goes.[5]

My grandfather died while my dad was in college. It was a difficult time for my dad, and he was angry with God for a long time over that. He didn't talk much about that time in his life, at least not to me. He did mention to me that after his father's death, he looked up at heaven and said, "Tell me now if it's true, God. Tell me if the whole thing about Jesus is true, because I'm not going to ask again." Then he said that in the Wesleyan way (even though he was Lutheran at the time) his heart was strangely warmed.

Many years later, my dad's heart let him down. He had a heart attack when I was in the seventh grade. I remember seeing him in the hospital with wires extending from him in seemingly all directions—I will never forget the day that I discovered my Superman to be mortal. Years later I told my dad that his heart attack is what inspired me to grow closer to the church. It was then that I knew life was precious and that we aren't here forever. In typical fashion, my dad quipped, "Son, if there had been any other way to get you to pay attention in church, I would have done it."

God has a strange way of communicating with us sometimes, and often he uses the unexpected in order to get his message across. Take, for example, the iconic "baseball scene" in *One Flew Over the Cuckoo's Nest*. Mac, played by Jack Nicholson, is a patient in a mental institution, living under the thumb of the dreaded Nurse Ratched. Mac is constantly testing the boundaries of who's really in charge in the institution, and his struggle comes to a head one night during a small group meeting. Mac requests to watch the World Series on the public room television. Nurse Ratched refuses, but puts the matter up for a vote, confident that her authority will not be challenged. She was correct. Mac, frustrated and furious, sits in front of the blank television set, impotent with anger, until he starts to imagine what the game would be like. He starts to call a play-by-play, describing the 1963 World Series between the Dodgers and Yankees. As he begins to describe Sandy Kofax's worst nightmare of a game-winning Mickey

Mantle homerun, the other patients are whipped into a frenzy. Nurse Ratched calls for them to settle down without success. Mac, armed with nothing more than a blank screen and a vivid imagination, was able to usurp Nurse Ratched's authority and created something out of nothing, offering the patients a system-challenging hope.

And the Score Is…

A portion of the original NBC Radio broadcast of Game 2 of the 1963 World Series was used in a scene from *One Flew Over the Cuckoo's Nest* in which the orderlies are listening to the game on the radio.

What systems need to be challenged in your community? Who needs to know the hope of Christ? How can your holy imagination create something out of nothing for the good of God's kingdom? What in your community do you tend to think of as "nothing" that God might be calling you to transform? Maybe some think it's "nothing" that some schools are underperforming. Some might think it's "nothing" that there's little access to affordable nutritious food in many urban settings. Some might think it's "nothing" that the affluent make mistakes, but the poor are criminals. But what might God want to make out of those "nothings"?

To take it a step further, what lies hold you back from believing that God can use you to create something out of nothing? In the 1999 sci-fi thriller *The Matrix*, everything humanity believed in and experienced was actually nothing. Machines enslaved humanity in order to use their biological energy as a power source. In order to keep humanity sedated, the machines connected people's brains to a life simulator called The Matrix. Like Plato's *Allegory of the Cave*, nothing humanity experienced while connected to these simulators was real. Their homes, workplace, food, and so on were a shadow of

113

ones and zeros inside a massive mainframe. Humanity was literally stuck in a system.

Neo, the hero of the story, seems to be a normal, everyday guy, but soon he starts to get Internet messages from someone named Morpheus saying, "The Matrix has you." Neo agrees to meet Morpheus in what seems to be an abandoned building, and Morpheus offers Neo a red pill or a blue pill. He says, "You take the blue pill, the story ends. You wake up in your bed and believe whatever you want to believe. You take the red pill, you stay in wonderland, and I show you how deep the rabbit hole goes." Neo takes the red pill, and discovers that his life is nothing more than a simulation. Throughout the movie, Neo, Morpheus, and Trinity fight the machines for humanity's freedom. At the end of the movie, Neo is killed while in The Matrix and therefore dies in the real world. Through Trinity's love, Neo is brought back to life, but as he awakens, he sees the world differently. He can see The Matrix for what it is—a lie. And now, instead of seeing walls and doors and windows, he sees only computer code—a computer code that can be manipulated in order to free humanity from captivity. Neo isn't Jesus, but he is the savior of humanity (and the machines too, if you stick around long enough to see the whole trilogy). Neo—The One, as he is known— experiences a death and a resurrection in order to free humanity from the lie it's been told.

SETTING THE MOOD

Color plays an important role in *The Matrix*. Scenes taking place in the Matrix have a green tint (as in a computer screen), while scenes in the real world have normal coloring. The fight scene between Morpheus and Neo, which is neither in the real world nor in the Matrix, is tinted yellow.

Sin leads us to believe we are powerless and unable to make a difference in the world for the kingdom. Remember, the problem with sin is that it's half right. We are powerless on our own, but with God's help, we can and do and are called to make a difference in the world for God's kingdom. When the Holy Spirit opens our eyes to see, we see that because of what Jesus has done, we are free and empowered to do God's work here on earth. This power rests with God, and not us. Through God's grace, the Holy Spirit offers us God's power to create something out of the nothing that sin offers so that one day all might know the grace, mercy, and love of God.

What are some broken systems in your community? How can your holy imagination bring healing?

A Monstrous Fear

Don't fear, because I am with you;
don't be afraid, for I am your God. – Isaiah 41:10

Our Hollywood Jesus doesn't always have to be a grown-up, you know. Jesus said, "Let the little children come to me, and do not stop them; for it is to such as these that the kingdom of God belongs" (Luke 18:16 NRSV). If the kingdom belongs to children, how might they understand our Hollywood Jesus? Several years ago I took my daughters to see *Monsters, Inc.* during its rerelease in the theaters. I noticed at first that they were watching the movie through their fingers because the opening scene is intended to make you think that something scary is about to happen. It's dark, things are moving in the corners of your vision, and a great looming shadow appears in front of the window…and then you realize the whole thing is a training exercise in an endearing, funny-looking monster world.

Suddenly a frightening scene becomes very comical. If you've seen this movie as many times as I have, you'll notice that this opening scene actually tells us the whole narrative of the movie, which is about the transformation of fear into laughter.

We are all too familiar with fear, aren't we? Fear appears early in the beginning of the story of humankind, when the man and the woman in the Garden of Eden eat the fruit of the tree of the knowledge of good and evil, and they hide when they hear God coming. The man says, "I heard your sound in the garden; I was afraid because I was naked, and I hid myself" (Genesis 3:10). What was once a loving relationship between God and humanity has now been changed by fear. You can hear this in the man's words: "I heard your sound in the garden." God's evening walk in the garden, which was once eagerly anticipated, now sounded thundering and ominous. Instead of being filled with a desire and love for God, humanity was now fearful of God.

It is very difficult to love someone you fear. Salvation rooted in a fear is a life rooted in the Fall. As believers, we are instructed to approach God with holiness and humility. When we pray, we do stand before an Almighty God who hung the stars and raised the mountains, and one day we will stand in judgment before Christ, but this should not fill us with fear. We will stand before Christ, who loves us enough to have given his life for us, and that is good and hopeful news! God took the fear that was birthed in sin in Genesis 3, and he offered himself in the person of Christ to transform that fear into love.

In the *Monsters, Inc.* town of Monstropolis, the monsters' city is powered by children's screams. It is their source of electricity. Monsters use special doors to sneak into children's rooms, scare them, and collect their screams in yellow power cells. Fear is a commodity. But one day an unafraid child sneaks into the monster world, and turns fear on its head—it just so happens that monsters are terrified of being touched by children or anything in the human world. In a comical twist, the monsters have been told to assume that children are dangerous and deadly. Really, the monsters' fear of children is a fear of the unknown. Most of us fear what we don't know, and I think fundamentally this is where any fear we may have about God originates. But when we read the scriptures and hear how God put on flesh and walked among us, to heal us and to challenge us, our fear and trepidation is transformed into praise and thanksgiving.

One evening my daughter woke up with the croup, and she was up most of the night. It was a pain, and I was frustrated because really the only thing you can do at 1:00 a.m. with a croupy child is to put them in the bathroom and run the hot water to make steam. As I was sitting in the bathroom with her, in my frustration, the Holy Spirit put a prayer of thanksgiving in my heart. I suddenly thought about what a blessing the hot water was, and how sad I was for some who don't have this luxury. Then the hot water ran out, and I started to panic again. Then I remembered that I could take my daughter outside to breath in the cold air. Again the Spirit brought me to a place of thanksgiving. I did nothing to earn or deserve this brisk, cold evening, but it is exactly what we needed. My fear of watching her struggle for each breath was transformed into a prayer of thanksgiving as we rocked under the stars.

A MAN OF STATURE

Sully in *Monster's, Inc.* is named after Lawrence Sullivan "Sully" Ross, former Texas governor and president of Texas A&M University (1891—1898). Students on campus place coins at the feet of Sully's statue for good luck on exams.

e end of *Monsters, Inc.*, the monsters' world is transformed when they discover there is something more powerful than fear—laughter. In fact, they discover that children's laughter generates ten times more energy than their screams, which changes their whole way of doing business. This is the story of our faith. Time and time again, when God appears, his words of greeting are, "Do not be afraid, for I am with you" (see Isaiah 41:10). When we are alone, footsteps sound ominous and scary, but when someone is with us, the darkness doesn't seem so dark. Jesus said, "Whoever welcomes a child welcomes me" (see Mark 9:37).

Not only are we called to have a deep love of God, we are also charged with loving each other and living in community. The monsters' fear of children seems silly to us because it's not our fear. We know that children aren't poisonous…mostly. Living in community helps us understand that we all have fears of some sort. A child's fear of monsters in the closet may sound silly to us because it isn't an adult's fear, but some of our adult fears, like the economy or success or status, may sound silly to children. Just because your fear isn't my fear, doesn't mean it deserves to be silent. Living in community is a blessing because we can give voice to each other's fears and begin to heal them. For my part, I would rather climb Mount Everest than go to the dentist. When the time comes, I break out in a cold sweat, I have trouble breathing, my body tenses up…it's ridiculous, I know. But when I come home from the dentist, my wife always says, "I'm proud of you," and I know it sounds silly, but hearing those words is so very important to me. I am able to face that fear because I know that, on the other side of it, Christie will always be there to give me encouragement.

You see, the opposite of faith is not doubt—the opposite of faith is fear. God is calling us to let go of our fear and live in faith that God will keep his promise to be with us. With a love of God and a love of neighbor, our fears are transformed into prayers of thanks-giving and praise, like a cold, brisk evening that brings healing, like an adult who says to a child, "I know you are afraid of the dark, so I want you to know that I'm here, and it's going to be okay." Like the child who says to the adult, "Dad, I know you lost your job, but I'll still play with you." Like God who puts on flesh and says, "Don't be afraid. Don't be filled with worry. Will worry add a minute to your life?" (see Matthew 6:27). May the hands that cover our eyes be transformed to hands opened to receive the grace of God, our Lord, our Judge, our loving Messiah.

What are you afraid of?

What are some ways you might overcome your fear?

Can you describe a situation where fear was transformed into joy?

THE GOSPEL ACCORDING TO YOU

With the eyes of your heart enlightened, you may know what is the hope to which he has called you.
    – Ephesians 1:18 NRSV

Hollywood Jesus takes on lots of different forms. He might have long hair and a beard and walk around with sandals. He might wear clown makeup or have the ability to sing killer rock songs. Hollywood Jesus might roam the pride lands or wield a lightsaber or seem as simple as someone with nothing in his hand.

If you were to offer a version of Hollywood Jesus, what would the story be? How is God speaking to you? Is God calling you from within the music you play? Is God calling you from within the numbers you crunch? Is God calling you from within the students you teach or the employees you lead or the children you raise? "With the eyes of your heart enlightened, you may know what is the hope to which he has called you" (Ephesians 1:18 NRSV). Each one of you has a purpose, and it is a purpose renewed with each breath you take.

Not only is God offering you purpose but he has given you gifts to fulfill that purpose. Maybe you've heard the cliché—"God doesn't call the equipped, but equips those he calls." There is a YouTube video that gets me every time. It shows two children opening Christmas presents. The little boy, with the help of his younger sister, opens the package to reveal that it is a Nintendo 64 Video Game System, and he just comes unglued! Life is easy when God gives us the kind of gifts that fill us with joy and happiness and peace (and video games).

But I also know a family who was overjoyed at the news that the first granddaughter would be born in several months, and so they planned their Christmas activities so that the mother-to-be could be congratulated at the evening church service. But what they didn't know was that this young mother had been to the doctor for a routine check-up before heading home for the holidays, and the doctor had found only silence. There was no heartbeat. When she got home, she listened to the words of congratulations from family and friends, and she said that each word of congratulations was a well-intentioned knife that continually cut out her heart. Several months later, she discovered she was pregnant again. Anxious, she went back to the doctor and heard a strong heartbeat! Her story is one that ends well, not just because she had a healthy child but because she now has a very rich experience, which helps her identify with young mothers who have lost children. She has a perspective that I will never fully grasp. Please hear me—I am not, and would never, suggest that God caused her miscarriage, but she has inherited a powerful perspective to help others who are wounded.

Paul wrote, "I pray that the eyes of your heart will have enough light to see what is the hope of God's call, what is the richness of God's glorious inheritance among believers" (Ephesians 1:18). God has given us gifts. We are God's heirs. Some gifts are full of joy and wonder—the ability to teach children, the ability to create artwork, the ability to save lives. Some gifts are full of lament and sorrow—the ability to help someone through depression because you know what it's like to live through that darkness, or the ability to lead someone through alcoholism because you yourself at one time admitted that you were powerless over alcohol. Whether we receive a gift of joy or a gift of sorrow, both can become rich experiences that help us understand our calling and purpose. God gives us purpose, and God gives us gifts so that this purpose may be fulfilled.

I hope that *Hollywood Jesus* has offered you a glimpse of the many ways we are called to be imitators of Christ through the gifts God has given us. There is a great power in realizing the calling God is offering to you. "I pray that the eyes of your heart will have enough light to see...the overwhelming greatness of God's power that is working among us believers" (Ephesians 1:18, 19). The same power that raised Christ from the dead is given to us by grace through faith. It is the power to change a person's life, not with a bolt of lightening, but with a patient ear and compassionate word. It is the power to end poverty, not with heavenly trumpets, but by opening your wallet and your heart and your mind and investing in education. It is the power to save a life, not by spilling water from a rock like Moses, but by offering a hand to someone saying, "Can I treat you to lunch? You haven't seemed yourself lately. Need to talk?"

Hollywood Jesus isn't about what Jesus looked like or figuring out which Gospel story is best to portray on the silver screen. It isn't about winning a box office war or making a nice family movie. It's about connecting with Jesus, our Lord, the Christ, the one through

ɔd was pleased to reconcile all things, including you and
about discovering that Christ is at work through the music
we wɪ.e and the games we play with our kids. It's about learning
that everything is a matter of faith, and God equips us to share that
faith. You might not ever be Luke Skywalker, but you can be Luke
Jackson. With God's help, you can change the world because all
things are possible through the Christ who lives within you. Our job
as Christians is to continue God's story. We don't have to be clever
or funny or original. We just have to continue to tell the good story,
and the good news is, it's already been told. Amen!

*Which movie throughout this study was most meaningful for
you to consider? Why?*

*Which movie could you live the rest of your life not thinking
about ever again? Why?*

*At the beginning of this study, what did Jesus "look" like to you,
and how has the image changed through the stories you've heard?*

NOTES

CHAPTER ONE: FROM SCRIPTURE TO SCRIPT

1. "Superstar," Andrew Lloyd Webber and Tim Rice, *Jesus Christ Superstar*, original Broadway debut October 12, 1971.
2. The original 1986 Polygram VHS of *Jesus of Nazareth* featured the full, uncut series in four VHS tapes.
3. Romans 1:29–32.
4. Matthew 5:21–22, 38–39, 43–44 NRSV.
5. Ryan Buxton, "*Birdman* Screenwriters Discuss the Film's Ambiguous Ending," *Huffington Post*, November 25, 2004, http://www .huffingtonpost.com/2014/11/25/birdman-ending_n_6219290 .html.

CHAPTER TWO: THE JESUS OF NOW... WHENEVER "NOW" IS

1. If you really want to dive into the "wibbly-wobbliness" of time, check out Matt Rawle, *The Salvation of Doctor Who* (Nashville, TN: Abingdon, 2015).
2. *Ben-Hur*, directed by William Wyler (USA: Metro-Goldwyn-Mayer, 1959).

3. "Strange Thing Mystifying," Andrew Lloyd Webber and Tim Rice, *Jesus Christ Superstar*, original Broadway debut October 12, 1971.
4. See Luke 22:19, Luke 17:19, John 11:43, respectively.
5. See Matthew 21:12, Matthew 12:10, Matthew 23:27, respectively.
6. See Luke 22:20, John 18:36, and Matthew 28:19, respectively.
7. See John 13:1–17, Matthew 14:13–21, Matthew 20:28, respectively.
8. "The Temple," *Jesus Christ Superstar*, Andrew Lloyd Webber and Tim Rice, *Jesus Christ Superstar*, original Broadway debut October 12, 1971.
9. "What's the Buzz/Strange Thing Mystifying," Andrew Lloyd Webber and Tim Rice, *Jesus Christ Superstar*, original Broadway debut October 12, 1971.
10. "Gethsemane," Andrew Lloyd Webber and Tim Rice, *Jesus Christ Superstar*, original Broadway debut October 12, 1971.
11. Monty Python's *Life of Brian*, directed by Terry Jones (USA: Handmade Films, 1979).
12. Ibid.
13. Chalcedonian Creed, adopted in A.D. 451 at the Council of Chalcedon.

CHAPTER THREE: THE GOSPEL ACCORDING TO…

1. *The Matrix*, directed by Andy Wachowski and Lana Wachowski (USA: Warner Bros., 1999).
2. "I'm Free," Pete Townsend, *TOMMY*, Track Records, 1969.
3. Tatooine, Hoth, Coruscant, Alderaan, and Naboo.
4. Bethlehem, Nazareth, Capernaum, Cana, and Jerusalem.
5. Mike Ryan, "Harrison Ford's Complicated History with Han Solo," Huffington Post, November 9, 2012, http://www.huffingtonpost.com/2012/11/08/harrison-ford-han-solo_n_2097347.html.
6. United States Environmental Protection Agency, "Municipal Solid Waste," February 28, 2014, epa.gov, accessed June 8, 2015, http://www.epa.gov/osw/nonhaz/municipal/.
7. *The Lord of the Rings: The Fellowship of the Ring*, directed by Peter Jackson (USA: New Line Cinema, 2001).
8. *The Lion King*, directed by Roger Allers, Rob Minkoff (USA: Walt Disney Pictures, 1994).

CHAPTER FOUR: EVERYONE HAS A STORY

1. *Cool Hand Luke*, directed by Stuart Rosenberg (USA: Jalem Productions, 1967).
2. Attributed to Saint Francis of Assisi (1181/1182—1226).
3. "Plastic Jesus," Ed Rush and George Cromarty, *Here They Are! The Goldcoast Singers*, World Pacific Record, 1962.
4. Ibid.
5. *The Matrix*, directed by Andy Wachowski and Lana Wachowski (USA: Warner Bros., 1999).

Acknowledgments

I am so thankful to share this study with you, but this study would not have happened without some very special people. I first have to thank my wife, Christie, and my lovely daughters Isabelle, Annaleigh, and Cecilia for sharing me with the ministry in general and this study in particular. I have to especially thank Chuck Long and Adam Darragh for helping me think through how important the camera is for the stories we tell. Thank you to Jay Grant who was my best friend and movie-going buddy throughout my childhood.

I must also lift up my colleagues in ministry and the churches I have served. Thank you to Reverend (Obi-wan) Ken Irby, who supports and challenges me every step of the way. Thanks to Reverend John Robert Black for loving me even though The Lord of the Rings is better than *Star Wars*. I must also acknowledge the support of my colleagues in the Louisiana Conference of The United Methodist Church and the grace I have received from the churches I have served. I need to especially thank The Well United Methodist Church for offering me grace as their pastor.

I am so thankful to Abingdon Press for offering me this opportunity. To the team: Susan Salley, Ron Kidd, Alan Vermilye, Tim Cobb, Marcia Myatt, Tracey Craddock, Camilla Myers, Sally Sharpe, Sonia Worsham, and Nancy Provost. I also must lift up Lori Jones for making me sound better than I deserve—you have a gift, my friend.